CHRISLAM

Fred DeRuvo

Chrislam

Copyright © 2012 by Study-Grow-Know

All rights reserved. Written permission must be secured from the publisher to use or reproduce any part of this book, except brief quotations in critical reviews or articles.

Published in Scotts Valley, California, by Study-Grow-Know
www.studygrowknow.com • www.rightly-dividing.com

Unless noted, Scripture quotations are from The Holy Bible, King James Version.

Images used in this publication (unless otherwise noted) were created by the author and are from clipartconnection.com and used with permission, ©2007 JUPITERIMAGES, and its licensors. All rights reserved.

All Woodcuts used herein are in the Public Domain and free of copyright.

All Figure illustrations used in this book were created by the author and protected under copyright laws, © 2012.

Cover design by Fred DeRuvo

Cover image: © Franck Thomasse - Fotolia.com

Editor: Hannah Richards

Library of Congress Cataloging-in-Publication Data

DeRuvo, Fred, 1957 –

ISBN 0983700672
EAN-13 978-0-9837006-7-8

1. Religion – Comparative Religion

Contents

Foreword:	....	5
Chapter 1:	June 26, 2011	7
Chapter 2:	Chrislam…What?	14
Chapter 3:	Babylon's Modern Frontier	22
Chapter 4:	Watering It Down	36
Chapter 5:	Islam Gains Ground	40
Chapter 6:	Muslim Brotherhood	49
Chapter 7:	The Bible vs. the Qur'an	59
Chapter 8:	Butterball Caves In	71
Chapter 9:	Unequal Protection	81
Chapter 10:	All-American Muslim	86
Chapter 11:	Is Mr. Obama a Muslim?	90
Chapter 12:	Bridging the Gap	95
Chapter 13:	The End	103

Do not answer a fool according to his folly,

lest you yourself also be like him.

– Proverbs 26:4 (NET)

Foreword

It is quite annoying – to say the least – when I read of movements that try to blend Christianity with other religions, as if the old lie that "all roads lead to God" is somehow true. The implication is that there is a great deal that Christianity shares with other faiths. These alleged shared values are enough to make people want to lead the march to bring the world of Christianity together with other faiths so that all will become one.

It annoys me because I know that the only way a person can arrive to this point is by essentially ignoring the bulk of God's printed Word – the Bible – or by allegorizing it severely. For centuries, people have interpreted the text of Scripture based on what I perceive to be faulty hermeneutics. That may sound arrogant, but consider the fact that if we approach the Bible with any less of a belief than that the entirety of it is God's Word to humanity, then we are doomed. We are doomed to misread and misunderstand His Word throughout, from Genesis to Revelation.

This is certainly nothing new as people have been attempting to literally rewrite His Word since it was brought together by the Holy Spirit. They have done so through omission and through addition. They have watered down and filtered out. Too many people have deigned to see themselves in the position of deciding what God means when they have not even taken the time to fully understand all of His Word in the first place!

The only possible way that Christianity and Islam (or anything else) have any connection whatsoever is by *removing* the biblical Jesus from the picture. Short of that, He must become so watered down that His personality and character no longer resemble His authentic character and personality as revealed to us in His Word.

This is – tragically – what people have done and what they continue to do. They substitute Scripture with their own favorite platitudes, somehow based loosely on Scriptural truth, but even then they have robbed the Word of its power and potency!

Chrislam is another mark of the enemy of our souls. It is another notch on his belt. In his efforts to divide and conquer, Satan has been very busy succeeding in this by doing the opposite: *uniting as one*.

Christians need to be so aware of the wiles of our enemy that we are never surprised. We must be two or more steps ahead of him and we *can* be *if* we are willing to rely on the God who lives within us in the form of the Holy Spirit.

Now more than ever – in these last days – we cannot take the chance of falling asleep. We cannot take our eyes off our Lord for one moment! We must be about the Father's business, and that includes being fully aware of the error that the enemy is attempting to use to pervert the *visible* Church. Fortunately, Satan will *never* be able to touch the *invisible* Church. Unfortunately, he has a field day with the *visible* Church. These are the actual churches, the actual people who attend these churches, and the pastors who minister to those who attend, some of whom are not authentic Christians, but merely *professing* ones.

The visible Church is in trouble because it is slowly being overtaken by Satan and his demons. In the process they are defeating and claiming souls. These souls need Jesus. Authentic Christians need to be aware of the danger that Satan creates. Then we need to warn those who are being seduced by that danger. Finally, we need to present truth wherever there is error. God will be blessed and fully glorified because of it. Where do you stand? Are you with God or with man?

Fred DeRuvo, March 2012

Chapter 1

June 26, 2011

The date noted as the title of this chapter was the day when numerous churches throughout the United States came together in a celebration of what came to be known as *Chrislam*. In short, Chrislam is a celebration of two different faiths (sometimes three) in what many hope to be a unification of religion in the coming days, and that celebration *must* include elements of Islam (hence, *Chrislam*).

Approximately 70 individual churches (and one seminary) chose June 26, 2011 to celebrate not diversity, but what they believe to be *unity*. Those churches ranged from Lutheran, to Unity, to Episcopalian, to Churches of Christ, to Methodist, Congregational, and even at least one Baptist.[1]

One must stop to ask: *exactly what do the religions of Christianity and Islam have in common?* That question is the most important question to ask in order to understand the Chrislam movement. The movement itself began through the efforts of a very well-known pastor of a very large California church and has resulted in another group coming into existence in order to oversee the movement as well as its progression.

Chrislam intends to *marry* Christianity *with* Islam. For this to occur there must be an elimination of major orthodox aspects of Christianity. Why? Without the removal of these doctrinal aspects upon which Christianity is founded, Islam cannot, nor will it participate. It is interesting to note that Islam itself is not being asked or expected to give up or set aside tenets that may in fact be objectionable to Christianity. Instead, it is *Christianity* that is being re-created in order to become palatable to Muslims. Why does this alleged *need* exist? Why are there people who believe that Islam needs to be catered to, invited, as it were, to become part of the religious landscape we know of as Christianity?

Imagine Christianity trying to shape itself so that any real differences between it and one of the cults completely evaporated. What would the result be? No Christianity. In order for Christianity to become partnered with any other religion or religious institution, Christianity would need to change. If it changed, it would cease to be Christianity. It would become something else, fused with whatever it was trying to blend or merge with. If that happens, does not a problem exist? It would exist only for Christianity.

---

[1] http://www.nowtheendbegins.com/blog/?p=5441 (10/15/2011)

There are many groups – cults, schisms, etc. – that have literally nothing in common with Christianity, yet they are always endeavoring to be seen as Christian. This is something they crave and it is understandable. Who wants to be said to be part of a cult or a fringe group? Is it any wonder then why many of these groups try so hard to be accepted as Christian?

Most Christians – at least, those who take their Christianity seriously – are aware of even some of the most basic differences with other groups and cults. Even for those who cannot pinpoint it (through lack of study), they instinctively know that there *are* differences, if for no other reason than they have heard that those differences exist.

Yet, with respect to Islam, the growing mentality is that Islam's god, Allah, is equal to Christianity's God, Jehovah. Islam's prophet Muhammad is equal to or greater than Jesus in the sense that Muhammad came *after* Jesus; therefore, he was Allah's final prophet.

We will endeavor to discuss a number of the major changes that are currently taking place on the religious horizon. They are not simply relegated to the area of Chrislam.

Beyond this, we are seeing an increase in the adoption and belief of the PostTrib Rapture position, the belief that the Rapture will occur, but it will take place at the end of the Tribulation period, as Jesus returns. Coupled with this, we often see the belief that eternal salvation is not as secure as one might think. Many within the area of PostTribulationism believe that salvation can be lost. The reason for this is that "once saved, always saved" is often associated with the PreTrib Rapture position believed to have first been espoused by Darby and made popular by Scofield.

There are some interesting, albeit dangerous, changes that are occurring within Christendom these days. Why is that happening? We'll look into it.

In one sense, we may ultimately find that the reasons for Chrislam coming into existence are the same reasons why the PostTrib Rapture position and the ability to lose one's salvation stem from the same pot. What do we do with that? Most importantly, what does the Bible say about it?

This is where it can get exhausting because we all know that for every position held by someone, they normally go back to the Bible for their proof. But what kinds of proof do they believe they have and how do they arrive at that proof?

As they say, proof is in the pudding. We need to be absolutely certain that what we believe is as close to biblical reality as possible. This takes a great deal of study, discernment, and prayer. Never forget that. You cannot simply read my books and arrive at a conclusion. You *must* always return to Scripture. You are responsible for what you believe. The best I can do is share with you what I believe to be true and why I believe opposing viewpoints are incorrect. I could be wrong. Obviously, I don't believe that, yet I am aware that I do not know everything about everything. I endeavor to approach God and Scripture with that perspective.

Much of the vitriol we hear today unfortunately comes from opposing sides, and they are over issues of Eschatology or something else that is really peripheral to the area of salvation. Chrislam directly affects what people believe in relation to salvation, and that is why it is important to understand what Chrislam stands for and if it has any Scriptural basis at all. If it does not, then it needs to be tossed out completely. If it *is* Scriptural, then no amount of protesting against it will amount to anything.

So why am I including other areas besides Chrislam that even delve into the area of Eschatology in this book? Aren't they outside the area of salvation? Yes, they are; however, in some cases, they are *connected* to salvation, as in the case of PostTribbers and their belief that one can lose salvation. Not all PostTribbers believe this, but from my experience, it seems that a large percentage of them do.

We need to dissect these areas as they relate to salvation and we need to try to figure out what is correct. It takes a good deal of study, prayer, and above all things, *patience*. We can too quickly arrive at what we believe to be a correct position and then look at others as enemies. People are not our enemies. Paul makes this clear. The enemies of our soul are Satan and his demons. Paul states that "*we wrestle not against flesh and blood, but against principalities, against powers, against the rulers of the darkness of this world, against spiritual wickedness in high places*" (Ephesians 6:12).

We often forget this and we tend to look at people with whom we disagree biblically as enemies, when in point of fact, if they are wrong, they are wrong because they're listening to the wrong entity. By "listening," I do not mean actually hearing. I mean that they have fallen under some type of deception that has caused them to believe the wrong thing. They also very often become stalwart in their opposition to and their denigration of people who hold opposing viewpoints. They tend to come to the conclusion that those who do, for instance, hold to the PreTrib Rapture or eternal security are completely deceived and therefore should be treated as lepers. This is not Paul's admonition. Though he does say that those who preach another gospel should be accursed (cf. Galatians 1:8), he is *not* saying that we should do the cursing. He is saying that the person should be accursed and the obvious conclusion is that God will do the cursing.

We need to treat people – even those whom we believe to be incorrect – as people who are yet salvageable. There are many who are not saved and who think they are, and there are many who do not have correct doctrine at their disposal, but think they do.

Let's consider what Jude says with respect to this. "*But ye, beloved, building up yourselves on your most holy faith, praying in the Holy*

Ghost, Keep yourselves in the love of God, looking for the mercy of our Lord Jesus Christ unto eternal life. And of some have compassion, making a difference: And others save with fear, pulling them out of the fire; hating even the garment spotted by the flesh" (Jude 1:20-23).

Notice that Jude's approach is complete humility. What I tend to see with people who believe they have arrived doctrinally is a strong sense of pride. They would, of course, disagree with that assessment, yet it is difficult to ignore it.

I have been called a heretic. I have been told that unless I repent of my PreTrib Rapture position, I'm going to hell. This is prideful to say the least, because my beliefs in the area of Eschatology do not necessarily affect my salvation. It is only when I replace the biblical definition of salvation with something else that my own salvation is affected.

For those who believe that the PostTrib Rapture is *the* way and that the PreTrib Rapture is not only *not* the way, but it is the only view that is born of hellish deceit, they begin to see people like myself as purveyors of lies and deceit. Because of this, I am seen as the enemy of Christianity and of Christ. The reason for this is because these folks do not believe that I am doing anything to prepare people for the coming Tribulation period.

They believe that I am actually providing a license to live any way they want because they are "saved," therefore nothing matters. We will all join Jesus in heaven. Because I am guilty of not helping people understand that the Church will go through the Tribulation (because ostensibly, the Church needs to be purified), I am guilty of peddling another salvation, one that is not true. Therefore, I should be accursed.

This is a huge jump, yet more and more people make it daily, viewing the PreTrib Rapture person as the enemy. This works out well for Satan because while I am being blamed, he goes about unnoticed.

So what can we say to all of this? We can go back to Scripture and see if we can narrow things down and provide a correct understanding of what the Bible actually says to us. We can do this not only in the area of Chrislam, but in the area of Supersessionism.

In both cases, salvation needs to be clearly understood. We cannot move on from there until we understand it to the best of our ability. Even then, we must humbly move ahead realizing that because of our fallen natures and finite minds, we may not understand things as well as we could or should.

So let's begin with a hard look at Chrislam; how it came about, what it means, and what it hopes to accomplish. From there, we will also look at a few of the trends like Supersessionism that have come to the fore and how they are affecting the way people look at Christianity and what God is doing in the world.

It's going to be an interesting journey as you travel the pages of this book. While doing so, please remember that I am a guide – a fallible guide. Consider my words against Scripture. Always begin and end with God's Word. That is the best way to stay on the right path, especially in these dark days in which we are living.

Chapter 2
Chrislam...What?

The idea of something called "Chrislam" is patently offensive to me. It is offensive because of what it *means* and what it seeks to *achieve*. It is literally a blending of elements of Christianity and Islam. Jewish rabbis are thrown in for good measure, it seems. Of course, the idea of blending Christianity with anything else is not only preposterous, but anti-biblical. It goes against what Jesus Himself stood for and who He said He was and *remains*.

Unfortunately, this movement that has come to be known as Chrislam began as a result of a severely watered-down understanding of Christianity and salvation in the first place. There is really no other way to describe it. Popularized by Rick Warren and Robert Schuller, it has grown to become a worldwide phenomenon in many circles.

It is not my intent to ridicule, denigrate, or castigate Rick Warren (or anyone associated whom I mention in this book). Unfortunately, it is impossible to write this book without mentioning names as it would become way too confusing. With that in mind, please understand that I am naming names to avoid confusion and because I'm quite certain that Rick Warren is very proud of his efforts and that what he has done and is attempting to accomplish is publicly verifiable.

More than one person has referred to people like Rick Warren as "love gospel preachers." They emphasize God's love to the complete exclusion of His judgment, as if it is non-existent. To these individuals, God's wrath is a completely antiquated view of God because it is derivative of religious mythology of ages past where God was *feared* above all things. The fact of the matter is that God should *still* be feared, even by authentic Christians.

Some may say that this is what Warren and others are referring to – this notion that God is in the heavens just waiting to find someone doing something wrong so that He can zap them! First up, if that was the case, that's all God would be doing each and every day because there are plenty of individuals on this earth who constantly live on the other side of His Law. Second, when I say God should be feared, it is like saying that a child has a healthy respect for his/her parents.

Fearing God even as His adopted child (through the only salvation available in Jesus Christ) does not mean that I walk in abject fear of Him zapping me or taking my life if I do something wrong. However, at the same time, if/when I do fall short I recognize that God has every right to be angry with me. More often than not, though, He is not angry with me, but disappointed. This is why we are to *confess* our sins to Him. This puts us on the same page with God with respect to the understanding that our sin is anathema, while we ourselves are *not* anathema.

I have said it before and will now say it again. When people arrive in heaven through their death, they will *not* go up to Jesus, slap Him on the back, and say, "*Yo Jesus! What's happening?!*" This kind of disrespect will not even be heard (or thought) of in heaven.

Jesus is our Friend, *yes*. But He will also *always* be our older brother *and* our Master if we take seriously the concept that He is Lord over all. As Lord, He decides what happens to those people who have dedicated their lives to serving Him. It's really that simple.

In the "olden" days, the elder son was essentially the head of the household when the father passed on. As such, this older son became the one who was in charge of what occurred within that household. He had the right and duty to decide for his siblings what role they would have, what jobs they would fulfill, and how the household would run. Sure, they could object, but it would normally amount to nothing. They had the choice of remaining in that household, under the direction of the eldest son, or they could leave. If they left, they also left their "inheritance."

This is the way it worked then and this is the way it works with Christians now. There are plenty of people who are part of the visible church and who are in it for themselves. Never having had any type of truly authentic salvation experience (as described in John 3; we're not referring here to ecstatic or ethereal experiences, but the event itself and what transpires because of it), they grow upset when things don't go their way. They may object to the way the particular local church they are part of does things and may be the type of person who wanders from church to church because of it. They also may be the type of person who tries to make solid inroads into their local church for the sole purpose of having things done *their* way. In any case, many of these people leave the church over issues that have nothing to do with the fundamentals of the faith.

People like the above often gravitate toward those types of churches where there seems to be a great deal more freedom: freedom to do, say, and live a certain way, as well as freedom to *believe* a very watered down version of the gospel. They do this because it *feels* good to them. They see many within that church as being very "happy" and they like that because they inadvertently believe that this is what being a Christian is all about: being *happy*. It isn't. Being a Christian means being saved ultimately from the fires of hell (something else people don't like to hear about) and, while here on earth, serving our Lord and doing whatever He expects/calls us to do without compromise or complaint.

Not long ago, Mr. Warren addressed the convention of the Islamic Society of North America, and in doing so, made a few interesting comments: *"Before we 'shake your hand' in responding to your letter, we ask forgiveness of the All-Merciful One and of the Muslim community around the world."*[2]

This type of comment confuses me. Does Mr. Warren actually believe that there are two gods somehow, or is he merely using the familiar moniker "All-Merciful One" as an indication that he also sees God in those terms, as Muslims do?

Second, why does Mr. Warren believe that Christians (for that is what he ostensibly represents) need to ask forgiveness of the Muslim community? What have *we* done to them that requires forgiveness? Shouldn't it be what Muslim extremists have done and are continuing to do throughout the world to those who are *not* Islamic?

---

[2] http://www.nowtheendbegins.com/blog/?p=1366

Not long after this conference, roughly 70 churches and one seminary throughout the United States entered into what they believe to be *"ecumenical reconciliation between Christianity and Islam."*[3]

Again, I have to ask the question, *why*? Why is it necessary that Christianity bow to Islam? That is essentially what Rick Warren is wanting and encouraging to occur. Because of this, we are seeing more churches that are coming round to believe that Jesus is actually in the Qur'an. This is the basis of wanting to reconcile because it is thought that if Jesus is actually in the Qur'an, then there is at least something that Christianity has in common with Islam, and if that is the case, then there is certainly reason enough to reconcile because maybe Christianity and Islam are closer than we think.

I have received numerous letters and e-mails from Muslims who attest to what they believe to be the fact that Christians and Muslims worship the same God. They simply call that god Allah, while Christians call our God Jesus. Islam denies that Jesus is God, however.

The problem with this type of assertion is that it tends to (or tries to) remove the walls of partition between Islam and Christianity. In doing so, the Person of Jesus is made to be something He is not. The Christians who join in with this type of worship wind up not only believing a lie, but have become the victims of terrible deceit.

In order to assess the true meaning and intent of Chrislam, we must go back to its roots. Those roots take us all the way to Atlanta, GA. *"The concept of Chrislam, now embraced by such preachers as Rick Warren and Robert Schuller, appears to have emerged from a program on the meaning of 'love your neighbor' at Grace Fellowship Church in Atlanta, Georgia[.] 'In 2001, like most Americans, we were pretty awakened to the true Islamic presence in the world and in the United States,' says Jon Stallsmith, the outreach minister at Grace Fellowship.*

---

[3] http://www.nowtheendbegins.com/blog/?p=1366

'Jesus says we should love our neighbors. We can't do that without having a relationship with them.'

"Stallsmith maintains that a rapprochement between Muslims and Christians can be achieved by the fact that Jesus is mentioned twenty-five times in the Quran.

"The Chrislam movement has gained impetus by statements from President George W. Bush and that Christians, Jews, and Muslims all worship the same God and by Rick Warren's reference to Isa (the Muslim name for Jesus) in his prayer at the inauguration of President Barack Obama. Only 30 percent of Americans have a favorable view of Muslims, according to a Pew Forum poll. At the same time, more than half the country says they know 'not very much' or 'nothing at all' about the Islamic faith. 'The recent political developments and the fact that we're fighting two wars in Muslim countries should sharpen that need to know how to talk to these guys,' Stallsmith insists[.] 'We want to find peace, reconciliation around a scriptural understanding of Jesus'."[4]

The reason people can come to believe that Islam and Christianity have more in common than not is solely because the average person has no real clue what Islam stands for and what its adherents believe. For that matter, too few Christians today actually know what they believe and how to prove it from Scripture. As one individual states succinctly, *"Jesus in the Quran is neither the only-begotten Son of God nor the Messiah who was divinely appointed to restore the House of David. He is rather viewed as a prophet who was appointed by Allah to prepare mankind for the coming of Mohammad."*[5]

People tend to look up to individuals like Warren and Schuller. Since Warren was essentially directly tutored by Schuller, then it is easy to see the connection between the two individuals and why they think alike in a number of theological areas.

---

[4] http://www.nowtheendbegins.com/blog/?p=1366
[5] http://www.nowtheendbegins.com/blog/?p=1366

In the case of one church that allegedly participated in a Chrislam service, they deny the accusation and have stated as much on their website. They also state the reason for what they believe is misinformation about them and their activities: *"We believe this situation stems from MDPC hosting a seminar, several months ago now, called Jesus in the Quran. The JIQ seminar seeks to equip people to better understand the religion of Islam. For the record, MDPC has not preached a sermon series linking Christianity to Islam. Likewise, we have not offered Sunday school classes in which we teach the writings of Mohammed. Furthermore, we have not placed copies of the Quran next to our pew Bibles. These accusations are fundamentally untrue."*[6]

The difficulty here is in their statement that they hosted a seminar in which they dealt with the subject of Jesus in the Qur'an. As noted, Jesus in the Qur'an is a completely different Jesus. They do not explain their purpose in hosting the seminar, nor did they explain what they thought about the Person of Jesus *as presented* in the Qur'an. If they are helping people understand how the Qur'an opposes orthodox Christianity, that is wonderful, but again, they did not say that's what their intent was, so we simply do not know.

I recall when I attended a conference for pastors a few years ago. I attended one particular lecture by an Old Testament professor who said that we don't need to "offend" Muslims by telling them that we (Christians) do not worship the same God. The word "Allah" simply means "God" in Arabic. That much is true. However, it is clear that the god that Muslims worship is *not* the God of the Bible, and their simply using the term that means "God" does not change that.

I came away from the seminar a bit disappointed simply because it seemed as though we as Christians needed to bow to the terminology

---

[6]

http://www.mdpc2.org/cms/index.php?option=com_content&view=article&id=314&Itemid=1222

that is common to Islam. In doing so, it would seem to me to be more confusing to the *Muslim*, quite possibly causing him to believe that there are commonalities between Christianity and Islam when none actually exist. In that case, why convert to Christianity?

To me, it is no different from worshiping with someone from Jehovah's Witnesses or Mormonism. They use similar terms to describe their beliefs and the latter especially believes that they are the true Christians and the rest of us have missed the boat. How is it possible to gather for worship with individuals whose belief systems are so different from that of orthodox Christianity? This is what people like Warren, Schuller, and others have been attempting to do, and what they wind up with is a religious New Age movement, alleging that Jesus is the Head of that movement, when in point of fact nothing could be further from the truth.

What we are seeing with the growth of Chrislam is nothing less than a modern day Babylonian system of worship where all gods are worshiped. However, the God of the Bible has always been left out of that system.

Chapter 3
Babylon's Modern Frontier

Modern Babylon is growing by leaps and bounds right in front of us, but so far, not many are aware of it. People by nature do not like to go against the grain because they will then be seen as *unpopular,* or worse, bigoted. Who wants that? We want to be accepted by our peers and do not want to be seen as outsiders. Heaven forbid we are seen as having no love for our neighbors even when disseminating the truth.

The problem is that we often mistake loving people *for going along* with them, even if it means giving up things that we know to be true. We justify this by saying that it is ultimately for *their* sakes that we are doing that because we don't want to offend. We become so caught up in not wishing to offend, we wind up saying *nothing* about the true gospel of Jesus and the fact that He is the only One who can actually save anyone from their fallen state, whether they are Jewish,

Islamic, Buddhist, or something else entirely. Under the guise of not wanting to offend, we end up *hiding* the power of the cross to save the lost, which makes us completely ineffectual. Is this what you want? I doubt it, but we need to be careful because Jesus said that those who are ashamed of Him He will be ashamed of before His Father (cf. Matthew 10:33; Mark 8:38; Luke 9:26). It seems contradictory to say that we love people so much we are willing to hide the truth from them so as not to "offend."

We can seek to justify ourselves all we want, but when it comes down to it, we *are* ashamed of Jesus, so we give into the peer pressure to not preach the true gospel. We wrongly believe that we will "soon" or "eventually" tell them the truth about Jesus, and in the meantime, they will see the truth in our *lifestyle.* Your lifestyle needs to backup your words, not the other way around.

Unfortunately, here's what they will see: someone who is weak and has caved into the peer pressure around him. This type of weakness will be seen as belonging to someone who is either not quite sure what he believes or *does* believe that there are enough commonalities between orthodox Christianity and Islam that it is fine to worship together.

How can we do that? More importantly, how can we hold our head up after that knowing that we have essentially *denied* Jesus' authority, His headship, His deity, and His salvation by allowing Allah to share the stage with Him? There is really no excuse for that.

What I find interesting is that many individuals who encourage movements like Chrislam also eventually wind up believing that all people will be saved. While this is normally termed *universalism*, they rarely state it as such because they are aware that most people have at least some vague idea of what universalism is all about and would disagree with it out of hand.

Chrislam

Rather than play their hand immediately, they prefer to suck people into their system or movement in the hopes of getting them used to the idea that Islam and Christianity are similar and that the Jesus of the Qur'an is the same Jesus of the Bible. Once they have gotten people sucked in, it will be very difficult for them to leave.

When it comes to that point, you will often begin to hear people saying things like, *"I believe in Jesus but that's for me. You hold Muhammad...near and dear and seek to emulate him."* This is sadly becoming part of the visible church. In this case, Muslims are more faithful to Allah than many who profess to be Christians are to God. If anything, you will *never* hear a Muslim say that back to you. In fact, I find it

fascinating that in places like England, Christians have actually been arrested for "hate speech" because of discussions they were in with Muslims. When the Christian lovingly yet firmly held their ground that Jesus is God, those Muslims went to the "lack of free speech police" and the Christians were arrested. This is not only tragic, but wrong.

For orthodox Christianity, it is absolutely impossible for it to be somehow blended into something that is becoming known as Chrislam. If that was the case, then there would be virtually no difference between Christianity and Islam or any other religious system. Jesus' statements that reflect His own deity or the fact that salvation is through Him alone would take on new meaning and essentially wind up with no meaning because they would be taken to mean whatever a person wanted them to mean.

This is the big problem, however, because most people see Christianity as a system that people come to believe in or place their faith in. These people do not understand that Christianity at its root is a relationship with Jesus Christ, God the Son.

Now, to be sure, there are several pastors who have come to Rick Warren's defense, stating without equivocation that Warren does not support Chrislam and is not part of that movement: *"Let me be very clear: Pastor Rick Warren does not believe in, promote or validate chrislam on any level. I have worked for Pastor Rick for the past 6 months, I have met with him on multiple occasions, I listen to him preach every weekend, I have read every book he has written, I have followed his ministry closely for almost 20 years."*[7]

Warren himself has stated, *"The so-called 'Chrislam' rumor is 100% false. If the guy who started this libelous myth, or anyone else who passed it on, had obeyed our Lord's command (Matt. 18:18-20) to come directly to me, and then asked what I actually believed – they would have been embarrassed to learn that I believe the exact opposite. As a 4th generation Christian pastor, my life & ministry is built on the truth that Jesus is the only way, and our inerrant Bible is our only true authority.*

"As an evangelist, I spend much of my time speaking to non-Christian groups. **You cannot win your enemies to Christ; only your friends, so we must build bridges of friendship** *and love to those who believe differently so Jesus can walk across that bridge into their hearts. Besides, it is not a sin, but rather COMMANDED by Jesus that we love our*

---

[7] http://www.christianpost.com/news/pastors-answer-does-rick-warren-endorse-islam-52833/

enemies. In the past 10 years, Saddleback Church has baptized over 22,000 new adult believers – simply because we express love to those who don't know Christ yet."[8] (emphasis added)

The problem may then stem from Warren *himself* and his seeming cooperation *with* and deference *to* Islam. As noted, he began one speech with an apology to the "*All Merciful One.*" Others have also indicated that they do not believe you can truly love someone without having a relationship with them, and Warren certainly seems to echo that sentiment in his comments quoted above.

Warren states categorically that you cannot win your enemies to Christ, only your friends. This does not seem to jibe with Scripture on any level. Jesus was not worried about making *friends*. He was concerned for people's eternal welfare and that concern prompted Him to do and say things that many of us would see as *unloving* and even *judgmental*.

Regarding the idea that we are to build bridges of friendship to the lost based on love, we need look no further than the parable of the Good Samaritan, which seemingly supports this concept. But we don't really even need to look that far beneath the surface to determine the truth of the parable and whether it speaks to building friendships or simply loving by filling a need at the time.

It appears plain enough from that parable, found in Luke 10:30-37, that this particular man who traveled the road and came across someone who had been attacked and robbed did not *know* the man. In fact, he had no relationship with him at all. Yet, unlike those who had seen him and walked by him without stopping to give him aid, this particular man – the Good Samaritan – *did* stop and not only tended to his wounds, but brought him to an inn – a place where he could recover. He also paid for the man's time there and promised

---

[8] http://www.christianpost.com/news/pastors-answer-does-rick-warren-endorse-islam-52833/

the inn's owner that on his return, if the man owed anything, he would reimburse him for that.

The two men were complete strangers and it is likely that the wounded man never actually met the man, either before or after the incident. Apart from being told that he a stranger had shown concern for him, he may not have been aware of this stranger's kindness and love.

In another biblical example of Jesus loving people, we see the time He talked with the woman at the well in John chapter four. There, Jesus took the time to sit near the well because He was tired from His journey. A woman happened along and He asked her to provide Him with something to drink. The reality here is that Jews did not associate with Samaritans, so Jesus was doing something that was not the norm.

This woman and Jesus did *not* have a friendship, or any other type of relationship, at all. It was the first time they met and Jesus set her free by telling her the truth about herself and pointing the way toward salvation. That Jesus took the time to step outside of existing norms and talk with this woman proves that He loved her.

How about another example of how Jesus showed His love for someone without being in relationship with them? The thief on the cross is one more example of Jesus' love for someone whom He did not personally know. In Luke 23, we learn how Jesus was illegally tried and convicted of blasphemy. We read about how Jesus was scourged and how He was brought to the place of His execution. Once there, we learn that the two thieves who were to die with Him both accused Him and reviled Him. We also learn how one of those thieves had a change of heart and asked Jesus to remember Him when He came into His Kingdom.

Jesus stated that the man would be in paradise that day. He was essentially telling the man that because of his belief and faith in Him (Jesus), salvation was given to him. Jesus did not have a relationship with that man either.

In fact, throughout the entirety of the New Testament and especially in the gospels, we see example after example of Jesus *loving* people and not necessarily building bridges of friendship with them. We see where Jesus took the time to pray for people, to feed people, to care for the sick and infirm and, most importantly, to tell people about the Kingdom of God. He likely knew *some* of these people, but it's just as likely that the majority of people He did not know.

Again, here is how Rick Warren views loving people: *"You cannot win your enemies to Christ; only your friends, so we must build bridges of friendship and love to those who believe differently so Jesus can walk across that bridge into their hearts."*

It does *not* seem that this was how Jesus did things. Jesus met needs, and from those needs He was able to free people from their bondage, whatever those bondages happened to be. For some, it meant He chased off demons. For others, He healed illnesses. For still others, He fed until they were filled, and with all of them, He spoke of God's love.

Jesus performed the miracles He did for two reasons. First, it provided proof of His credentials. Second, it was hoped that those miracles would create a desire within people to receive salvation. There is no way that Jesus could have built relationships or friendships with all the people to whom He ministered. Yet He certainly loved all of them without exception, even those He knew would turn Him over the religious authorities and those who would deny Him three times before the cock crowed.

There were numbers of people who walked away from Jesus without ever turning to Him for salvation and the gospels are filled with those accounts. Loving people does not guarantee they will eventually receive salvation. Loving people merely shows them a side of God that they likely had not experienced prior.

I could spend years loving people by building relationships with them and *waiting* for a time to tell them about Jesus and His love for them. I could hope that my life would serve as an authentic messenger of the gospel, opening doors for me to speak to them about God's love and His salvation. I can do what Rick Warren says he does, but where might things end up? Put simply, relationship evangelism does not really work. What happens is that Christians enter into friendships with unsaved people and think that one day they will be able to tell their friend about Jesus in *clear* terms. They may think that though they will be gentle, they will one day unhesitatingly share the gospel. They also believe that when they do, the person on the receiving end of it will either accept it with gladness or reject it and they will still remain friends. The emphasis is on *friendship*.

Rick Warren says you can't win your enemies to Jesus; only your friends. This simply does not pan out in Scripture. In fact, I guess if we take Warren's words as truth, then we must admit that the apostle Paul was doing it *incorrectly*. Paul did not take the time to enter into relationships with people. He spent his time preaching and evangelizing the lost. He was hoping to take lost souls and introduce them to the only One who could provide salvation: *Jesus*.

I guess Paul should have taken the time to draw people close to him by *becoming* their friend first, and then after enough time had passed so that those new friends began to trust Paul through many evidences of "love," Paul would be able to spell out the gospel to them. Instead, Paul essentially went into new cities throughout Asia Minor, and wherever he went he would go to the Jews first with the gospel.

Often they would reject him and his message, forcing him to go to the Gentiles, who would often receive what the Jews had rejected.

When I read words such as those uttered by Rick Warren, I immediately think of *platitudes*. Warren believes that as Christians enter into relationships with people – relationships built on friendship and love – that Jesus will be able to *"walk across that bridge into their hearts."* The quoted part is nothing more than a *platitude*. It makes for great copy and pulls at people's heartstrings, but in the end, does nothing. It does nothing because the responsibility to convert is actually on Jesus, not on the individual Christian.

I believe that in the types of situations Warren speaks of, Christians wind up dumbing or watering down the gospel because they have gotten to know someone and do not want to risk offending them or driving them away. It is very difficult to witness to people who are close to you. I personally believe people like Warren are missing the mark.

I've listened carefully to Rick Warren on shows like Larry King and elsewhere. On such shows, he is normally with someone else who has a completely different world view. What I've noticed is that Warren *does* seem to try to find common ground, but more often than not, he also winds up throwing Christianity under the bus because in his efforts to win friends, he is losing the battle to win souls.

I fully realize that Jesus opens people's eyes to the truth, and He can do that with or without us. However, I really do not see in Scripture where those who wound up following Jesus did so *because* of a relationship or friendship He had built with them. He came to set the captive free, and it was very clear from His words and His works that He wanted desperately to do this as quickly as possible for people.

Notice that when the rich young ruler came to Jesus and asked Him what he must do to be saved, Jesus told Him. In Luke 18, this young man approached Jesus because I'm sure he thought he was already saved. I'm of the opinion that he wanted accolades from Jesus, not a true critique of his situation.

Because of this, he was saddened to learn that he actually *lacked* something! How could this be, he thought, after everything he had done since he had been a young person?

Jesus pointed out that in spite of all the things the young man thought he had done correctly, none of it was good enough because his heart was sold out to riches. That was his god. In order to gain true salvation, the young man would have to leave his idolatry and come to God empty handed. He was unwilling to do that.

Now, suppose Jesus – afraid that He would have no real credibility with the young man – decided to skirt the issue when the man approached Him. Suppose Jesus thought it more important to enter into and build a friendship with this young man than simply tell him the truth straight out. What would that have sounded like?

It may have gone something like this:

Man: Good teacher, what must I do to be saved?

*Jesus: My, you're very polite. Thank you for calling me 'good.' That's just great. Being saved? Well, that depends. What do **you** think being saved means?*

Man: Well, I have done many things that I believe have helped me gain salvation, but I need to know if I have been on the right path.

Jesus: Very good; I'm glad that you're thinking earnestly of this because it is a very important subject. What things have you done?

Man: Well, I've obeyed the commandments since my youth. I have not lied, committed adultery, stolen anything, and I have always honored my parents.

Jesus: That is excellent. It is obvious that you take your vows to God very seriously. What else do you think you should do, if anything?

Man: That is the problem. I cannot think of anything else and that is why I have come to you today.

Jesus: You are very wise. I think you are on the right track and I believe God will reveal to you what you might be missing, if anything. You need to listen carefully to hear His voice.

Man: Really? So, I might be doing everything I can already?

Jesus: I think if you listen, God will direct you.

Man: Thank you!

Jesus: You're welcome. Let's continue this dialogue...

Man: Yes, let's!

So what's wrong with this picture? In this scenario, Jesus has *compromised* by not telling the man like it is in order that the man's eyes might be opened. We do this too often, and we can call it trying to develop a friendship or relationship with someone first, but in reality we do not want to scare them away. Ultimately, it would appear that we do not trust that God will be able to save them unless *we* do or say things correctly.

This brings us to another question. What does Rick Warren (or anyone, for that matter) mean by "loving" people? It is clear from Scripture that Jesus defined loving people by His *words*, His *lifestyle,* and His *actions*. We've already seen a few examples of the way Jesus loved as well as a great example provided for us by the Good Samaritan. It would seem – and I could be wrong – that for Rick Warren, as for many people, loving others means **getting along well with them**. Loving people means accepting them for who they are and what they believe as the basis of a relationship with them, then over time, *hop-*

ing that Jesus will *"walk across that bridge into their hearts."* But again, what does *that* mean?

In one interview with John Piper, Rick Warren stated a number of his beliefs without equivocation. He denied that he is a Universalist. He is not postmillennial. Warren also stated that Jesus is the only way. He continued to make declarative statements throughout the interview.[9]

Warren also emphasized the need to *love* people; however, in the interview, he failed to define love, which to many people simply means advocating a certain set of *emotions*. He *loves* people and his heart *hurts* for people.

Maybe Rick Warren and others like him are trying too hard to do things the world's way. Maybe they firmly believe that the best way to introduce salvation to people through Jesus is by becoming their friend first and allowing them to see how much they are "loved" (again, whatever that means), and then one day, they will be so overwhelmed with that love that they will have to turn to Jesus to receive Him.

This could be the way they are looking at it, but the reality still seems to be that their approach to spreading the gospel is far different from what Jesus and the apostles did. They preached. People heard. Some were convicted unto salvation, while others were convicted until their hearts became too hard to understand what that salvation truly meant. Their rejection of the Good News kept them away from God and His salvation.

Chrislam – whether it actually exists or not – seems to stem from people's desire to minister to members of Islam. Unfortunately, inviting Muslim clerics (Imams) and Jewish rabbis into a Christian ser-

---

[9] http://www.christianpost.com/news/what-rick-warren-believes-about-salvation-eternal-life-50610/

vice in order for each to take part in a communal service of sorts is not the best way to plant seeds of repentance that may lead to salvation. It sends the wrong message.

Whether Rick Warren began Chrislam or if he was merely *credited* with starting it is moot at this point. The fact of the matter is that Chrislam *does* exist, it is growing among the visible Church and it is unfortunate that the average church-goer is not more aware of the problem. But maybe they do not wish to be aware of it. This same problem has existed for some time with respect to the Emergent Church and its *encouragement* of the same types of things that are found deep within the confines of the secular New Age movement.

It would appear that few Christians really know what they believe and, just as bad, have very little discernment. The reason is that they do not open the Bible as often as they should to study and attempt to determine exactly what God says on a variety of subjects.

We need to be a discerning people. We need to know His Word. We need to understand exactly what it means to be a Christian and why being an authentic Christian separates us from the masses. This is not a point of arrogance. It is a point of fact, and while that fact can and does create contention, it also brings freedom to those who are willing to hear the truth: the truth about themselves, the truth about God, and the truth about the only salvation that has ever been or ever will be available to humanity.

Chapter 4

Watering It Down...

T ony Campolo is not the first to adopt a more...how shall we say?...*heretical* approach to the presentation of the gospel, and he certainly won't be the last. In many ways, Campolo tends to be the yardstick by which others measure themselves.

At first glance, the quote attributed to him in the one-panel comic above may appear to some to be one of those "oh wow" moments. The reality, though, is that all Mr. Campolo is doing is watering down the gospel by mucking it up in confusion. His implied point seems to be that if a person is a Muslim or Buddhist, Jesus could just as easily be living "in" that person as well as Christians. This does not square with Scripture, but that often means nothing to people like Campolo, who prefer ethereal-sounding verbiage to the solid truth of Scripture.

It unfortunately reminds me of the way Satan often approaches people. He builds truth into his lies, but in the end, the whole thing becomes a lie even though there may be a bit of truth within it. Look at what Satan said to Eve in Genesis 3. Take some time to read that chapter right now. I'll wait...

Okay, ready? He said, "Did God really say?" Then he proceeded to explain what God *really* meant. This is how people often gain an advantage over Christians who aren't really clear about God's Word. Eve presents a perfect example of that situation because she really did not fully comprehend what God had said, and this is evidenced by the fact that she added to God's original command by stating that God had apparently said that Adam and Eve could not only not eat it but they could not touch it. God had said no such thing. I'm sure Eve was probably thinking that eating and touching were the same thing, because if you're going to start touching something edible, it might not be too long before you start eating it too.

So to Eve's way of thinking, merely touching the fruit would result in death. She may have even thought that if she accidentally brushed up against it, she would die.

When people do not know and understand God's Word, the problem often begins. This was Eve's problem. She was not sure of God's Word, what God had literally said to Adam. Who knows, but maybe Adam got it a bit mixed up and added it, so then naturally Eve would keep it, thinking it was part of the original command.

If Adam was hanging around at that point while the Tempter was tempting Eve (and Adam likely *was* nearby), then you would think he would have taken the time to correct Eve, but he in fact said absolutely nothing through the entire event as he sat there watching it unfold right before his eyes. Great leadership on Adam's part...not.

So today, we are experiencing more and more people glorifying themselves by *changing* the Word of God to mean something it does not mean. Whether they add to Scripture or take away, in each case they wind up changing the meaning of it to suit their own beliefs and preferences.

This is exactly what is happening in the visible church today. People want to draw as many people to themselves as possible and they can do this most effectively by telling people what they want to hear. Paul calls this the process of itching people's ears (cf. 2 Timothy 4:3). People want good news. They want to know they are "okay," and they simply do not want to hear anything bad about themselves.

The rich young ruler proves that point. He came to Jesus for accolades, not constructive criticism. The fact that he went away proves that he was not ready to make a firm commitment to God, as he thought he had been doing all of his life. That was a major wake-up call to the rich young ruler, but he preferred being asleep. Unfortunately, he could not go back to that time of blissfulness when he thought he was doing everything correctly and would only hear praise from Jesus. He was thoroughly disappointed.

Are we like that? Are you like that? Do you come to God expecting "attaboys/attagirls" only to realize that your life has something missing or you do not love the way you should love? God doesn't show these failures in our life so that we can wallow in self-pity or begin to hate ourselves.

God shows us these things because He already knows what we will *become* when He is finished with us. He is simply providing direction to help get us to that finished point when the image of His Son will be permanently replicated within each of His children and there will be absolutely no sign of sin within us. That happens in the afterlife, but He works on it continually in the here and now while we are alive.

Chapter 5
Islam Gains Ground

We've talked for a bit about the problems that are infiltrating the *visible* church (otherwise known as Christendom) because of Islam. It might be a good idea to shift our focus onto Islam to better explain some of these problems that face the visible church, Christians, and the world at large. We need to determine what, if anything is wrong with Islam that would preclude it from being a viable part of a *free* society.

There are many who might be tempted to believe that Islam and Christianity are complimentary, much the same way that people believe that Judaism is fine and that Jews do not need salvation because Christianity essentially sprang from it. The problem can be summed up in the fact that Islam and Christianity are not complimentary at all. In fact, it's really like comparing Jesus to Satan. There *is* no real comparison because Jesus stands infinitely superior to Satan, Muhammad and Allah in every way.

That may certainly sound like a very harsh way to put things, but in the end, Christianity either stands alone or it is merely one of many religions. There are many who believe the latter – and that's their choice – but believing it does not make it so.

What we need to do is put both systems (for the lack of a better word) next to one another and from that perspective determine whether they mesh or repel. If they mesh to any degree, then we can go to the next step. However, if they repel from the onset, then it is clear that the distance between the two would keep them from ever coming to a point of agreement.

Eradicating Freedom of Speech
There are many difficulties with Islam. From the so-called prophet Muhammad, to the beginnings of his ideology, to the way in which he dealt with people who would not accept him as messiah and more, there are huge problems that are embedded in the timeline of history.

One of the larger problems is the more common tendency of Islamists to want to whitewash history as we know it. They wish to obfuscate the reality of Muhammad's life, attempting to present him as something he was most definitely not.

You see, the first thing Islamists attempt to do is destroy freedom of speech. They do this by working within a democratic system to create laws that will define any criticisms of Islam as hate speech. That in itself is tragic, yet it is occurring and has occurred in many places throughout Europe.

If Islamists can get laws passed that protect their religious ideology from being criticized or "defamed," then they have gone a long way in winning ground for Allah.

If we merely look at the situation in the United Kingdom, it becomes very clear that politically correct versions of Islam are routinely presented as fact. Those who would attempt to correct these misrepresentations are silenced with threat of incarceration.

Many people have already become subjected to this law and have spent time in Great Britain's jails because of it. All it takes is for some Muslim to complain that so-and-so said that Muhammad was a child molester, or a pedophile, or something as innocuous as the statement that he was not really a prophet and the person could be subjected to fine, imprisonment, or both. This is patently ridiculous!

What other group – religious or secular – demands these types of safeguards? I can think of only one other group, and they are found within the Gay and Lesbian community.

As a Christian, people use the Name of Jesus – my Savior and my Lord – as an epithet on a daily basis. They do so with impunity and do not care one iota if I am offended or not. More often than not they do this out of habit, not even noticing that they are saying it.

In America, atheists buy space on billboards to further their inane messages about the "myth" of Christianity or Jesus. They can legally do this because of freedom of speech. I can object if I want to, but they are under no obligation to remove the billboard sign because they are not breaking the law. The signs may make them appear asinine, but being asinine is not the same as breaking the law.

Redacting History

Textbooks throughout classrooms in America teach evolution as if it is a proven fact, when in reality, nothing has been proven. Evolution by its nature denies the existence of God, which is why people like it. I can complain about it if I want to, but schools are under no obligation to change their textbooks.

There are many ways in which abuse of some sort is heaped on Christians on a daily basis. We are expected to turn the other cheek because that's what Jesus taught, and never mind that there is a context behind His words that do not mean that I must be a doormat for people.

Christians do not go through the proper channels trying to pass laws that "protect" us from unreasonable criticisms. My Christianity is criticized on a daily basis. It is simply what the world does and there is no end in sight, at least not until Jesus returns. It goes with the territory.

However, where Muslims are concerned, they want the situation to be that no one can have the ability to criticize Islam, its founder, or their god. It is so asinine that it is difficult to believe, yet this is what organizations like CAIR (Council on American-Islamic Relations) do, and they work under the radar as much as they can.

If they aren't trying to get anti-criticism laws passed, they are promoting special situations to employers in the U.S. that relate to Muslim Americans. CAIR believes that Muslims should be given special privileges to pray or to wash their feet in ceremonial bowls in order to perform their religious rites throughout the day. What other religious group has these benefits?

It is one thing to ask for a day off for a religious observance, but quite another to force an employer to make room for a person's particular rules of faith. Again, Christians do not do this, yet it is fine for Islamists to do it.

ACT for America! has uncovered ways in which CAIR and other groups are changing history through textbooks. They work with the publishers of the textbooks to ensure that the history of their prophet Muhammad reads as they wish it to read, not the way his life was actually lived.

Muslims do not want it known, for instance, that Muhammad married a young girl named Aisha when she was merely **six years of age**. They try to fend off the label of pedophile by deferring to cultural norms at the time and by stating that Muhammad did not consummate the marriage until Aisha had turned the ripe old age of **nine**. However, even if that was the case, a girl of nine is still too young to be married.

Muslims also do not want people to know just how barbaric Muhammad was and how many people he simply murdered because either they did not receive him as messiah or he simply hated them. Muslims want the world to honestly believe that Islam is a religion of peace, and in order to accomplish this feat, they must find ways to present Islam in a very favorable light.

The average person who knows nothing of Islam will not notice the discrepancies in the textbooks and therefore will not be alarmed. Those who *are* aware of these falsehoods will attempt to bring the matter before the proper authorities and insist that the truth be known.

This is the way that radical Muslims work. They try very hard to pull the wool over the eyes of the public in order to present Islam as something that it is not. Once they accomplish this, any red flags evaporate in the minds of the average person. This then allows Islam to continue its encroachment to gain more ground. By the time people realize what has happened, it is often too late to push back against the rising tide and dominance of Islam. This is clearly the case in places like the United Kingdom, The Netherlands, Belgium, France, and numerous other places.

One of the more interesting things is the way in which Muslims attempt to obtain these special privileges. For instance, not long ago a number of Muslims were attending a Roman Catholic college. It was not long before they began complaining that they needed their own room that was completely devoid of religious icons and imagery because this was against their religious practices. As of this writing, no word on whether the college is going to acquiesce, but consider the ramifications of this.

Muslims are voluntarily attending a Catholic college. They knew it was Catholic when they applied and when they were accepted. Nothing was hidden and they likely toured the school before applying.

However, *after* they became students at the school, they began to exert efforts to make the college *conform* to their own personal religious perspective. By doing this, what happens is that they gain more ground ultimately for Allah.

If that college gives in and provides a room for these Muslim students, they will then be asked to do something else. If they give into that, something else will be asked, and it doesn't stop.

Eventually, Muslims do an Islamic make-over so that they wind up changing the appearance of something to make it become more Islamic. That is the intended goal.

Think of why Muslim students – who have nothing in common with Roman Catholicism – would want to begin attending that college in the first place. Why would they do that? They say it is because they feel "safe" there as opposed to simply being at some secular college with no religious affiliation. Unfortunately, I don't buy it because the incidence of hate crimes against Muslims in this country is virtually non-existent. There is no reason Muslim students should not feel safe. This reasoning of theirs is simply a ploy to artificially create a situation that puts them in the driver's seat.

In France, legislators attempted to push back against the use of veils over faces of Islamic women. Obviously, for a Muslim woman to have her I.D. or license photo taken with her face covered serves no purpose. Apart from the veil, there is nothing that identifies the woman at all. What is the point of even taking the photo?

So, Muslims rallied in protest saying that France's regulations regarding photographs for I.D. cards of any type violated their religious practices. France continued to push back and won, making it illegal for a woman to completely cover her face for her photo or even in public.

In this day and age of terrorism, it is not inconceivable to believe that radical Muslim *men* might take the opportunity to dress up as women in order to set off a strapped-on bomb. The burka offers great protection against seeing what is underneath because there is a good deal of space to have things on your person. Couple this with the anonymity of covering your face and it becomes an almost perfect disguise.

In another recent turn of events, a Muslim group visiting an amusement park was told that they were not allowed to wear long scarves or veils on the rides as this could cause injuries or even death if the fabric became caught in the mechanics of the ride. You would think the park had asked the women to appear in the nude! The situation nearly turned violent, with the Muslims becoming very agitated over this rule because again, they said it violated their religious obligations.

They were told ahead of time and seemed to have no difficulty with it. However, once they got to the park and attempted to ride on the rides and were told they could not with their scarves and veils, that's when things became heated.

Muslims like this count on people backing down. Most people do not want a fight. They don't want to have to deal with violence of any kind, so the civilized thing to do is give way to the person who is going off like a firecracker. Muslims count on this, and too often the Muslims themselves are not arrested when something turns ugly. It is the person who is on the receiving end of the Muslim's ire who is arrested.

This has occurred in Dearborn, MI too often because of the annual Arab Festival that takes place there. Both the mayor and the chief of police have bent over backwards to placate the Muslim community, and in so doing, Christians have been arrested, jailed, and even tried for crimes of disturbing the peace. This is in spite of the fact that Muslims were the ones who began acting violent toward the Christians, and there is a good deal of video evidence to support this fact. Fortunately, it was some of this same video evidence that brought about "not guilty" verdicts by juries of their peers.

This is the goal of Islam. It is to take over an area, dedicating it to their god, Allah. Once they have established themselves in one area, they broaden the scope of their insurgency so that the area is enlarged. Muslims will do this by any means necessary. They will use war if the situation permits, just like those areas in the Middle East. They will use a nation's own legal system to establish for themselves an ever-growing area of influence. They will simply "squat" in an area, acting as if they own it. As more Muslims come into that area, the population grows, and then one day a sign that says "Sharia Controlled Zone" goes up and people who are not Muslims do not go in. Muslims have won by default because they have successfully pushed out those who are not Muslim.

From that point onward, Sharia Law rules in that area and these neighborhoods are essentially let alone by law enforcement officials to do what they do under Sharia Law.

It really does not matter *how* they gain more ground. What matters is that they *do* gain as much ground as possible because the more ground gained, the sooner the sixth caliphate will commence.

What other group is able or allowed to do this? Christians are not allowed to set up their own communes or communities in which they become their own law and through which they ignore local laws and ordinances. It makes no sense, but since Muslims often react violently to things that they see as coming against them, people all too often back down and give in. This is exactly what Muslims count on to happen. They do not expect anyone to stand up to them and many simply do not.

Chapter 6

Muslim Brotherhood

Ever since I began writing on the problems of Islam and its encroachment on free society, I have received a number of emails and responses that attempt to portray *me* as the extremist. What I've learned, of course, is that the individuals who have written these responses to me are more than likely agents of disinformation.

Here is an example of what I have received. (I've left the grammatical and spelling errors in as I received it): *"What a lot of hogwash You generalize, and of course you inject your personal bigotry. You think*

Christianity is 'clean' of violence? It's funny that in most wars, both sides claim god is on their side. Your article is so taken out of context that it's not worth commenting on. All religions are cults. Maybe you should read Leviticus a little closer if you are a true believer. Most Muslims are good, hardworking people. They do not believe in violence. It's the radical extremists, just like in Christianity, that propagate violence. It's also a mob mentality, just like we can have her, that lead to violence. We see it happen after huge sporting events. As for Obama and sharia law... what planet are you on? Or you part of the wacky morons that believe that he's a Muslim, or not an American? You should be thankful for the USA that gives you the right to preach your lunacy. I put you right there with the American Nazi Party, Your right to preach BS."

At first glance, this appears to be from someone who might want to be classified as an atheist ("*All religions are cults*"). The problem, though, is that this particular individual is protesting a bit too much, and it's all in support of Islam. Notice how he laments that my "*article is so taken out of context that it's not worth commenting on*" yet he takes the time to do just that. In fact, it's obvious he couldn't wait to comment on my article.

I won't take the time to respond to the individual's comments line by line, but notice the statement, "*Most Muslims are good, hardworking people. They do not believe in violence. It's the radical extremists, just like in Christianity, the propagate violence.*"

This person has inadvertently given themselves away because of their less than intelligent comments. Though they attempt to pretend that they are affiliated with no religion at all (based on their throwaway comment that *all religions are cults*), the reality is that they spend the entire paragraph *defending* Islam while trying to shine the light on Christianity as if Christianity is the truly violent religion.

Note also the attempt to shut me up by calling me a *lunatic*, a *wacky moron*, and one who is *equal to the American Nazi Party*. These slams fully give this person away. He's not an atheist. At the very least, he's an Islamic sympathizer and at worst, a radical Muslim trying to wear the cloak of an innocent lamb.

This is exactly what Muslims do when they are cornered. That's their main defense: to go on the offensive by attempting to turn the tables on the person who brings out the truth about Islam.

If you have never read the books *Muslim Mafia* or *The New Muslim Brotherhood in the West*, I would strongly suggest that you do. It's interesting to note that CAIR has sued the publisher and author of Muslim Mafia because it brings out the truth about the Muslim Brotherhood and their plan to overthrow the United States. While this plan may seem completely far-fetched to the average and uninformed person, it is unfolding here in the West. Muslim Brotherhood and others like them take advantage of this mindset because it gives them a cloak of invisibility that allows them to work unnoticed by most people here in the United States. They love the fact that so many people here in the West are complacent and asleep at the wheel.

Allah is our goal, The Prophet is our guide, the Quran is our constitution, Jihad is our way, and death for the glory of Allah is our greatest ambition. - Muslim Brotherhood Credo.

The most famous saying of the Muslim Brotherhood is "*Islam is the solution.*"[10] What does that tell you? They are currently living the dream in Egypt and other parts of the Middle East, as well as in various places throughout Europe.

The Muslim Brotherhood is an extremely dangerous organization. Their credo above tells us without equivocation their plans and intents. This not only applies to America but to every other country

---

[10] Ghattas, Kim (2001-2-9). "Profile: Egypt's Muslim Brotherhood". BBC News

they can manage to become part of through infiltration. Unfortunately, though they are actually outlawed in numerous countries, the United States has yet to attach the label of terrorist to this organization.

The book *Muslim Mafia* explains in detail how the Muslim Brotherhood came to be, how it works, and what its goals are not only for the United States, but also eventually for the entire world. It is interesting to note that with the overthrow of Hosni Mubarak of Egypt, the Muslim Brotherhood has risen to the occasion and exerted its influence to replace the failed government of Mubarak. Though there have been and are attempts by others to keep Muslim Brotherhood from taking full control of that country, the results seem to be failing miserably.

According to the book, the Brotherhood's plan to Islamize America consists of five phases:

1. **Phase I:** Establishment of an elite Muslim Leadership, while raising taqwa - or Islamic consciousness - in the Muslim Community.
2. **Phase II:** Creation of Islamic Institutions the leadership can control, along with the formation of autonomous Muslim enclaves.
3. **Phase III:** Infiltration and Islamization of America's political, social, economic, and educational systems, forming a shadow state within the state... Escalation of religious conversions to ISLAM. Manipulation of mass media and sanitization of language Offensive to Islam
4. **Phase IV:** Openly hostile public confrontations over U.S. Policies, including rioting and militant demands for special rights and accommodations for Muslims.
5. **Phase V:** Final Conflict and Overthrow (Jihad).

It is important to understand that the Muslim Brotherhood is now in Phase III, but patience is key to their strategy. They are willing to wait "100 years" to achieve their subversive goal, as Alamoudi put it.

It is also important to understand that *"every major Muslim group in the U.S. is controlled by the Muslim Brotherhood."* This information is cited by veteran FBI agent John Guandolo who continues by stating, *"It's not just a loose network of people sharing a common ideology, he says but a centrally controlled and directed insurgency."*

"Members of the Group [attempt] to infiltrate the sensitive intelligence agencies or the embassies in order to collect information and build close relationships with the people in charge in these establishments."[11]

As time progressed, a number of situations arose that allowed our government to determine the truth about Muslim Brotherhood's plan for this country – the United States. A secret U.S. Brotherhood Charter was found in the possession of Brotherhood underboss and convicted terrorist Sami al-Arian.

There is the case of Ali "the American" Mohamed, a loyal member of the Muslim Brotherhood who emigrated from Egypt to spy for the Brotherhood in America. After failing to penetrate CIA OPS he infiltrated the U.S. ARMY as a sergeant and wound up at Fort Bragg training with U.S. Special Forces, where he obtained a secret security clearance. Although not a Green Beret, he worked alongside the elite Berets learning unconventional warfare and counter insurgency operations. The military trusted him, and before long he was teaching soldiers about the Middle East at the J F Kennedy special Warfare Center, where unbeknown to his superior officers, he was stealing classified military secrets. During weekends and other leaves he would travel to New Jersey to train al-Qaeda operatives in weapons and warfare tactics which they would later use against the country

---

[11] Ghattas, Kim (2001-2-9). "Profile: Egypt's Muslim Brotherhood". BBC News

Mohamed had sworn to protect. After his honorable discharge from the Army, Mohamed moved to Santa Clara, where he set up a communications cell for al-Qaeda while fronting as a computer Engineer. In 1995 he brought Dr. Ayman al-Zawahiri to California for a mosque fundraising tour, reportedly raising $1.2 million for the al-Qaeda Leader. A large chunk was raised at CAIR Founder Omar Ahmad's Mosque in Santa Clara, a key Brotherhood hub (Ahmad is employed as a computer engineer in the Silicon Valley). Five years later the Feds finally got wise to Mohamed, and after his arrest on terrorism charges he pleaded guilty to five counts of conspiracy for his role in planning the al-Qaeda bombings of the U.S. embassies in Africa.

The Mohamed case marked the first in a series of instances in which dangerous Muslim Brotherhood figures have successfully penetrated key U.S. Institutions.

The book notes that, *"We are in a battle of life and death, in a battle of fate and future against the Western hegemony. What is needed is the dismantling of the cultural system of the West. Al-Arian managed to penetrate the White House along with his pal ALMOUDI before federal authorities caught up with him. He pleaded guilty to terrorism charges, served time in jail and now under house arrest on separate contempt charges for refusing to co-operate in the SAFA group investigation despite a federal Grand Jury Subpoena.*

"'The Muslim strategy for change within incorporates the secretion of loyal brothers into political office' warns former FBI agent Sadla. Groups like CAIR, MPAC, MAS, the ISLAMIC INSTITUTE, and American Muslim Alliance have aided this project. Some recently founded AMT (American Muslim Task Force on Civil Rights and Elections or AMT) to promote candidates into public office and not just at the Federal level, but state and local levels as well.

"CAIR's Ahmad landed a position on the Santa Clara City library Board. He was a trustee for 10 years while CAIR launched its so called Library

Project, successfully targeting some 8,000 neighborhood libraries across the country with packages of books, videos and other Brotherhood propaganda for sanitizing ISLAM."

The book continues with information on additional situations perpetrated by loyalists to the Muslim Brotherhood: *"In Fairfax, VA, a Muslim traffic engineer who works for the county recently testified on behalf of the Radical Islamic madrassa run by the Saudi embassy during heated county hearing over the school's expansion. His testimony with an outpouring of 600 Muslim supporters, helped the Academy Win approval of its plan, even though it has been cited by the U.S. Government for promoting violence and intolerance through its textbooks and has acted as a breeding ground for terrorists, graduating even al-Qaeda operatives."*

While the Muslim Brotherhood is outlawed in other countries, the U.S. has not yet designated the group a terrorist entity or foreign threat, even though it has stated clearly that it supports violent jihad and is dedicated to replacing the U.S. with an Islamic Theocracy.

Juan Zarate, former Chief of the Treasury Dept. Terrorist finance unit, said, *"the complications [of] dealing with the Muslim brotherhood [is that] 'they operate [their] business empire in the Western World, but their philosophy and ultimate objectives are radical Islamist goals that are in many ways are antithetical to our interests. They have one foot in our world, and one foot in a world hostile to us. How to decipher what is good, bad, or suspect presents a severe complication. After 9/11 federal investigators noticed most leads traced back to the Brotherhood."*

Further, we learn that *"In 1981 ISNA was founded as 'a nucleus for the ISLAMIC Movement in North America.' Now the umbrella organization for the Brotherhood controls several front groups and hundreds of mosques and schools. It was an unindicted co-conspirator in the Holy Land Foundation Terrorist trial ending with a conviction in March*

2009. While CAIR enjoys more notoriety and is more visible in the media, ISNA is more venerable and ingrained in U.S. Society. Its predecessor, MSA, still serves as the main recruiting tool for the Brotherhood in the U.S."

Regarding MSA, it should be noted that they have 150 campus chapters and is one of the nation's largest college groups. CAIR Chief Nihad Awad got his start as an MSA activist at the University of Michigan.

In truth, what we are seeing (or not, depending upon how open our eyes are) is that because of the Muslim Brotherhood, militant Islam is spreading throughout the United States. Too many people still do not believe it, preferring to close their eyes to the onslaught.

One of the reasons people have a difficult time believing statements like this about Muslim Brotherhood and other radical Islamic groups is because of the public demeanor of many of those who represent Islam through the numerous organizations throughout America. These people are seemingly friendly, they dress in business suits, they carry themselves well and they have an educated background and speak English better than many who were born in the United States. How can these people be bad for America?

All we need to do is look at the old Roman Empire to determine how it fell and we quickly realize that the main reason Rome fell was due to its own inherent arrogance. Rome felt it was superior to the rest of the world, having conquered so many nations with seeming ease. How could anyone – much less a few rogue Germanic tribes of the north – gain an advantage over mighty Rome?

Whether it was due to actual arrogance, a refusal to see what was coming, or a combination of both, Rome did fall, though it took time.

Muslims can wait it out. They can work diligently once they are inside a country to quietly and consistently work to overthrow the existing government. They do this in many ways, but one of their best defenses is working within institutions that give them access to agencies and entities that create laws in America.

What is very interesting is that information has been slowly coming out that alleges that there is a definite influence of the Muslim Brotherhood in the Obama Administration. In fact, what's even more interesting is the name of at least one of the people who is making this charge. He is Canadian political activist, devout Muslim and self-described liberal Marxist, Tarek Fatah.

This past June, Fatah was quoted as saying, *"the religion of Islam is being used as a tool by a fascist force."*[12] Also interesting is what he said about the Muslim Brotherhood and the White House: *"Instead of bringing victory over the fascist forces of the Muslim Brotherhood, we now recognize that their infiltration is right up to the American White House, but we can't say that."*[13]

In many ways, the Obama Administration – whether intentionally or unintentionally – has been one of the greatest assets for the phenomenal growth of radical Islam in this country. Mr. Obama's alleged connection with Bill Ayers and ACORN is common knowledge. Beyond this, not long ago, under the direction of the White House, ordered the removal of all references to Islam in connection with any examination of Islamic jihad terror activity. The Obama Administration has now placed any investigation of the beliefs, motives and goals of jihad terrorists off-limits.

Obviously, whether Mr. Obama is a Muslim or not is moot. He **acts** like one because of his favorable attitude toward those of the Islamic ideology, and that's what matters.

---

[12] http://www.theblaze.com/stories/new-warning-about-muslim-brotherhoods-influence-on-white-house-from-liberal-marxist-muslim/ (11/20/11)
[13] Ibid

Islam is not going to go away. What needs to happen is that people need to become educated about Islam and what Muslims are working to bring about in the United States. It's happening right under our noses and most can't even smell it.

The liberal media won't address it, so don't expect them to do so. This leaves independent bureaus and individuals to bring the truth to the public. Along the way, there will be a fair share of agents of disinformation who will attempt to denigrate people into silence. It won't work because they are seen for what they are: Muslims pretending to be something else.

It is a disgrace that moderate Muslims are so quiet about the Muslim Brotherhood. Many have said they fear for their own lives. I'm sorry about that, but due to their silence they wind up aiding and abetting the Muslim Brotherhood and other radical Muslims. There is no excuse.

Let me also say that I am not in the least worried about any of this. It may seem as though I am, but I'm not. I know and understand that God has all things under control. That, however, does not mean I sit around and do nothing.

While I stand against the encroachment of Islam, I do so looking for opportunities to evangelize the lost; in this case, Muslims, whether they are moderate or radical. Whether they listen to me or not is up to the Lord and His willingness to open closed eyes to His truth.

Chapter 7

The Bible vs. the Qur'an

O ne of the most interesting aspects of Islam is found in the person of Muhammad. He was a man who lived in the A.D. 600s and whose life has inspired millions of people who desire to emulate him. In effect, since people often view imitation as the sincerest form of flattery, living your life with the same goals and purposes of the founder of Islam is the highest form of compliment to him.

But what about Muhammad? We have briefly discussed the fact that many within Islam have already taken up the cause of redacting history in order to show Muhammad only in a good light.

These efforts and mentalities have already taken their toll on numerous textbooks being adopted by school districts today. Islam endeavors to prove to people – even by lying – that Muhammad was a great man, a man who strove for peace by any means and one who lived as an absolute holy and devout man of Allah.

Because of this mindset within the leaders of the Islamic community, many of the actual details of Muhammad's life must be glossed over or eradicated altogether. Beyond this, the Qur'an – known to be the holy book of Islam – is said to be far superior to the Bible.

What about that? Is there any way to know whether or not this is true? Of course, each person will make their own decision about the Qur'an and the claims of those within Islam, but we will present what Islam presents about the Qur'an and will compare it with the facts surrounding the Bible, allowing you to arrive at your own decision. At the very least, it is hoped that you will desire to do greater research on your own.

According to Mir Zohair Husain, Associate Professor in the Department of Political Science and Criminal Justice at the University of South Alabama (2003), facts about the Qur'an are easily attainable. He presents many of them in his work *Islam and the Muslim World*.[14]

In the first section of his text, Husain presents a multi-paged table that compares Islam, Judaism, and Christianity. We will avail ourselves of this material throughout the remainder of this book as only one source of information. Pertaining to the Qur'an, Husain reports, Muslims are to believe that *"the Qur'an is God's last message to mankind and has been preserved in its original form to this day; was*

---

[14] Mir Zohair Husain *Islam and the Muslim World* (McGraw-Hill, 2006)

revealed to Prophet Muhammad by Archangel Gabriel; that God's revelations embodied in the Qur'an came to Muhammad over a period of 22 years (610 – 632 CE); and that in Prophet Muhammad's case, the Qur'an was his greatest miracle."[15] Beyond this, Husain tells us that *"the Psalms of David, the Torah (Hebrew Bible), Old Testament, and the Injil (Gospels of Jesus Christ) are not in their original form, and therefore do not contain the original Word of God."*[16]

So what we learn from these two facts is that the information contained within the Qur'an was culled from a 22-year-period of Muhammad's life. So in effect, the Qur'an quotes one man over a period of a few decades. This would be like having only the book of Proverbs for a holy text.

Note also that Islam has simply declared that the Judeo-Christian Bible has been corrupted and therefore cannot be trusted as being the very words of God. This is something that many groups (sects, or cults) do *if* they have their own text that they venerate more highly than the Bible.

Mormons do this because they include their Book of Mormon in the mix for Mormons. While Mormons are certainly allowed to read the Bible, they are taught that if the Book of Mormon seems to contradict the Holy Bible, the word of the Book of Mormon must supercede the Bible because it came *after* the Bible, making it God's latest (and presumably final) word to humanity.

The Jehovah's Witnesses do this as well with their New World Translation and other books produced by the founders of the Jehovah's Witnesses movement. Whenever something that either the Book of Mormon or New World Translation says appears to contradict the Scriptures, adherents are expected to discount the Bible in favor of the text that is connected to their particular religion.

---

[15] Mir Zohair Husain *Islam and the Muslim World* (McGraw-Hill, 2006), 47
[16] Ibid

Islam does this with the book they call the Qur'an. Again, though, in Islam's case, we have a book that covers a period of 22 years in one man's life.

The Bible, on the other hand, was written over a period of 1600 years and includes individual books by some 40-something authors. What is even more impressive is the amount of consistency found within its pages.

Yes, so-called higher critics have done everything they can to rip apart the Bible's integrity and veracity, but there is always an answer to their claims and the answer is always *rational*.

While the Qur'an contains 114 suras (or chapters), it is relatively small in size compared with the scope of the Bible. The Bible contains 66 individual books, and with the exception of smaller books such as Jude and Philemon, all are multi-chaptered. Of course, people still argue and will continue arguing over the veracity of the Bible.

It must be remembered that like other sects/cults, Islam's holy book – the Qur'an – came well after the life, death, resurrection, and ascension of Jesus, the Founder of Christiantiy and Creator of all things according to apostles Paul and John (cf. John, Romans, Philippians, Colossians, Revelation, etc.).

Muhammad himself lived from approximately A.D. 570 to 632. During his life, he came to be known as Allah's prophet, and the creation and spread of Islam began.

It is interesting to note that during Jesus' life He said and did many things that ultimately point to His deity. Jews, Muslims, and other non-Christians do not recognize Jesus as God. Many see Him as a good prophet or good teacher, but not God. Some say he was not even a good teacher, and still others deny that He actually lived but instead was merely a conglomeration of people created by a small band of individuals. In this case, Christianity would then be the only religion that was founded upon someone who did not exist. That in and of itself (along with the longevity of Christianity) makes claims of His non-existence spurious at best.

While the Qur'an mentions Jesus "*as one of Allah's great prophets and messengers,*"[17] this same book denies Jesus' deity. However, at the same time, the Qur'an does teach that Jesus performed miracles and attests to the fact that He was born of a virgin.

However, when we get to the part referring to the crucifixion of Jesus, the Qur'an denies that this occurred: "*They did not really slay him [Jesus], neither crucified him; only a likeness of him was shown unto them (4:157).*"[18] This means just what it says: that a likness – either an impersonator, vision, or ghost – died but not Jesus, as Allah is believed to have taken Him off the cross just prior to His death.

Yet the Bible tells us that Jesus willingly gave up His Spirit. "*Father, into your hands I commit my spirit*" (Luke 23:46). Muslims simply get around this by stating that the Bible has been corrupted.

Of course, the problem with the charge that the Bible is no longer in God's original words is that we must apply the same test to the Qur'an. It is historical fact that at one point the Qur'an had so many versions and translations that seemed to contradict one another that a group of Islamic scholars had to get together to eliminate many of these versions to narrow things down.

Patricia Crone and Michael Cook, on page 18 of their work *Hagarism: The Making of the Islamic World* (Cambridge, 1977), have this to say about the Qur'an: "*[The Qur'an] is strikingly lacking in overall structure, frequently obscure and inconsequential in both language and content, perfunctory in its linking of disparate materials, and given*

---

[17] Mir Zohair Husain *Islam and the Muslim World* (McGraw-Hill, 2006), 46
[18] Ibid

to the repetition of whole passages in variant versions. On this basis it can plausibly be argued that the book is the product of belated and imperfect editing of materials from a plurality of traditions."

Though Muslims believe that the Qur'an is the result of faithful recording of the teachings and sayings of Muhammad, it seems clear that this is not the case. Of course, Muslims would disagree, but given the fact that Muslims are taught not to read the Qur'an themselves in an attempt to discern its meaning but are instead encouraged to have an Imam (teacher) read the Qur'an to them and explain its meaning, one can only wonder how the average Muslim can attest to the Qur'an's veracity. It obviously comes down to what they are taught.

Many might say this same thing about the Bible, and yes, there are people who never open its pages. However, there *are* many who not only routinely open the pages of the Bible but study it for themselves in addition to listening to the teachings of others pertaining to Scripture.

On a number of things, Muslims and Christians agree. Both believe that Jesus ascended alive into heaven and will bodily return just prior to the time of world judgment.

Also, both the Bible and the Qur'an refer to Mary, the physical mother of Jesus. The Qur'an refers to her as Maryam, which is her Arabic name. One entire chapter of the Qur'an – chapter 19 – talks about Mary.

What is also fascinating is the fact that Islam is at the very least tolerated by many of the world's political leaders (including many within the United States) and, in some cases, even encouraged. This is likely due to the fact that either people simply do not understand what Islam is all about, or sadly, they are on the receiving end of large cash contributions to their campaigns.

But let's take a moment to learn about the "dos" and "don'ts" within Islam. Everyone is familiar with the Ten Commandments and most know that conservative Christianity – what I like to call *authentic* Christianity – rules out things like same-sex marriage, living together, sex prior to marriage, stealing, lying, cheating, murdering, etc. In fact, Christians get slammed today on many levels because of the fact that they cannot agree with the homosexual lifestyle or abortion, two hot-button issues in today's society.

While there are a few – this author can think of *one* – groups that have an extreme reaction toward members of the Gay and Lesbian community, even there, the people involved in these groups relegate themselves to carrying signs and shouting slogans. As far as I know, no one from these groups has done anything *physically* or even threatened to do something physically to either gays or the families of gays. This does not excuse their behavior, which is in many ways reprehensible without excuse.

But what does Islam teach? For some, it appears to be free of the type of negativism that seems to follow Christianity, but is it? Not long ago, I received an e-mail from someone as a response to one of my articles I had posted to my blog (www.studygrowknowblog.com).

The writer stated, "*i find you thoughts entertaining. you say that the quran promotes killing those that are not muslim. you say that Islam dictates how you live. you get angry at [another person] because he calls you an extreamest. here is something for you to think about. the christian bible stories and discribes what should be done to those who do not follow the christian way. the bible gives you the ten commandmants which tell you what you can not do, and if you do any of those things you will go to hell. you told col mohd that his entire religion was made of extreamists that will enslave and kill any one who isnt muslim, when in fact there just as many christian extreamists as there are muslim. and no im not muslim. but im definitely not a fan of your christian church either.*"

I've not changed anything or corrected any grammatical errors. It amazes me how often people will write trying to sound intelligent, yet their form of writing gives them away. It is very difficult to take someone like this seriously.

The person quoted fails to understand a number of things related to both Christianity and Islam. Beyond this, he seems completely unaware of the reason *for* the Ten Commandments as well as to whom they were originally given.

Please note that the person's real goal was to castigate Christianity by presenting falsehoods pretending to be truth. But if we simply travel back in recent history, it is easy to determine the nature of terrorism.

Nearly *all* terrorist incidents have been committed by people from Islam. While there are – admittedly – a few rogue individuals who *call* themselves Christians and who bomb an abortion clinic or shoot an abortion doctor with a high powered rifle, it is very, *very* clear that Muslims are the real perpetrators of evil in this modern world. Just because someone *says* they are Christian does not make it so. The so-called Christians who bomb an abortion clinic or murder an abortion doctor are very likely Christians in name *only*.

When the individual in Norway killed just under 100 people by pretending to be a police officer and stating on his social network page that he was a "right-winger" and a "Christian," only a bit of research debunks the belief that he was either a police officer *or* a Christian. In Europe, people routinely call themselves Christian because they attend church or because it designates a social standing.

Calling themselves a Christian does not mean they are, in the true senses of the word. For them, listing "Christian" on some piece of paper is the same as those of us in America listing "Caucasian" on some application or claiming to be "Protestant." It's what we identify with and that's it.

After more research, we learn that the shooter in Norway was a member of an extreme sect that has nothing to do with Christianity. In fact, it's an offshoot of one of the sects of the Roman Catholic Church – the Knights Templar – which is, for some reason, enjoying a type of resurgence in Europe, most likely due to the exponential growth of Islam there.

The worst part of it is that people like the one I quoted above seem more concerned about trying to defend the actions of those militant Muslims by pretending that the problem is not that big, as opposed to condemning their actions. As long as people like these exist, refusing to stand up to the routinely perpetrated evil of Muslims, they are just as bad, just as guilty, and it's as if they have committed those acts of barbarism themselves.

If I asked anyone to define what it means to be a Christian, they would probably list off a number of things that they believe Christians do (or should do) to qualify for being a Christian. I would then instruct them to read the third chapter of the gospel of John for the actual definition of what it means to become a Christian.

Anyone can be a Muslim one day and something else the next because being a Muslim simply means following a set of commands. Being a Christian is far different from any other religion on earth. In no other religion is a person "born again" or "born from above" as Jesus explains to Nicodemus in John 3.

Regarding some of the "dos" and "don'ts" of Islam, what are they? Let's take a few moments to look at them. Aside from the obvious, like not murdering, lying, and stealing, what are the Islamic laws?

1. **Homosexuality**: forbidden
2. **Nudity**: not allowed

3. **Pre-Marital Sex**: not allowed
4. **Adultery**: not allowed
5. **Divorce**: uses as a last resort
6. **Birth control**: allowed
7. **Gambling**: not allowed
8. **Politics**: entirely fused together in Islam with religion

Let's back up for a moment and talk about homosexuality as it pertains to Islam. Being homosexual or being part of the gay or lesbian lifestyle is forbidden if one is a Muslim.

In Islamic countries of the Middle East like Iran, homosexuality is swiftly dealt with and normally means death for the accused/convicted. The most common way of meting out the death penalty for homosexuality is through hanging.

When President Ahmadinjad visited the United States in 2007 and gave an address at Columbia University, he was specifically asked about his country's position toward homosexuality. He stated from his lecturn that homosexuality does not exist in Iran. This was met with disbelief and laughter. Later, a translator stated that Ahmadinejad's comments were misunderstood.

In some way, Ahmadinejad could have been telling the truth, at least as far as he thinks, because whenever a person is discovered to be a homosexual, they are executed. End of the "problem." However, Iran states without equivocation that it does not execute people solely due to their sexual proclivities. They are executed because of crimes *beyond* that of being homosexual, like rape, murder, or trafficking in drugs. However, this is questionable. *"Some Human rights activists and opponents of the Iranian regime claim between 4,000 and 6,000 gay men and lesbians have been executed in Iran for crimes related to their sexual preference since 1979."*[19]

Whatever the reality is in Iran and other countries controlled by Islam's Sharia Law, the reality here in America is far different. Not only is being gay not considered a crime (as sodomy used to be in the United States), but because of the efforts of numerous gay and lesbian groups, homosexuality is increasingly seen as normal.

Authentic Christians would have to disagree with the idea that homosexuality is normal simply because the Bible expresses a completely opposite view of homosexuality. While I'm aware of the arguments proferred by gays and lesbians that assert that the Bible nowhere condemns homosexuality as a normal lifestyle, it is clear to this author and many others that they are grasping at straws. Nonetheless, no truly authentic Christian that this author is aware of would want homosexuals executed for their sexual proclivities.

In fact, there are cities and areas within the United States where the things practiced should not be discussed openly. One such event is held annually at San Francisco's "Up Your Alley" where the things done in public should never see the light of day, much less be condoned and performed on the street somewhere. During this event, local politicians, authorities, and law enforcement look the other way, in spite of the fact that what occurs is normally relegated to the closed doors of a brothel.

Yet in spite of this, gay and lesbian groups routinely condemn Christianity as a group who stands in the way of normalizing homosexuality. What that means is that these groups want Christians to be quiet and remain quiet as far as their opinion toward homosexuality goes.

---

[19] To, Passed (February 4, 2011). "Iran: Uk Grants Asylum To Victim Of Tehran Persecution Of Gays, Citing Publicity". The Daily Telegraph (London). (11/21/11)

If Islam had its way in the United States, homosexuals would at the very least be imprisoned, fined, or whipped. In most cases, they would very likely be executed.

Chapter 8
Butterball Caves In...

When it came to my attention a few days before Thanksgiving that Butterball was now offering halal-compliant turkeys, I have to admit that I became a bit angry.

For those who do not know, meat that passes the "halal" test means that Muslims can eat it because it was ceremonially killed while the butcher called out the name "Allah." This may not seem to be necessarily bad because after all, don't Jews eat products that are Kosher? Yes, they do, but there is a huge difference. While Kosher foods are blessed by a rabbi, the food that is blessed and ultimately becomes Kosher is *never* mixed with food that is *not* Kosher. So if I go to the store and decide to buy pickles or butter or something else that is Kosher, I know it's been prayed over by a rabbi. I also know that this particular product was never mixed with the same product of a non-Kosher nature.

Butterball® turkeys have been a favorite in our household for decades. It's just what we ate, and after I married, I tried to keep that tradition alive and well.

Now, however, the folks at Butterball have decided that it is far better for them to cater to Muslims by making their turkeys – all of them that they produce – fully halal-compliant.

When it first came to my attention, I was concerned that it was some stupid hoax meant to hurt the sales of the Butterball Company, so initially, I ignored it. However, I then began reading about it and hearing about it from a number of sources, so I began to take it seriously.

Finally, I decided to hear it from the horse's mouth, so to speak, so I put in a call to Butterball corporate offices to hear for myself whether it was true or not. The woman I spoke with in Customer Service was very nice. I explained my concern and asked whether or not she could verify if Butterball turkeys were, in fact, halal-compliant.

She confirmed that the turkeys now sold by Butterball were halal-compliant. She also offered that they had been receiving phone calls "non-stop, all day" about the issue. I was glad to hear it. I explained to her how Islam works. They use every method at their disposal to *encroach* upon society. It doesn't matter if they're dealing with schools, political offices, grocery stores, or anything else.

Because of the nature of Islam, Muslims go through life asking for and expecting special privileges. These requests seem reasonable to most people, so they extend the privilege to them. What people *fail* to realize is that the catering to Islam *never* stops. Muslims know this and take full advantage of it.

Dhabihah is the process for making foods halal-compliant. What this means is that there is a special ceremonial process that the animals – turkeys, in this case – go through at the time of slaughter. Included in this ceremony is the calling out of Allah's name while the animal is being slaughtered. If this part does not happen, Muslims are not supposed to eat the meat from that slaughtered animal.

So here's what we have: Butterball is now catering to Islam so that the Muslims can now eat their turkeys during Thanksgiving, a celebration in the United States Muslims could not care less about the meaning and history of, though they benefit greatly from our nation. This means that *because* I have been made aware of this process, I cannot eat the turkeys, turkeys that I have been eating for years!

*"All Muslim scholars hold that mentioning God Almighty name at the time of slaughter is a must, they differed as to whether or not forgetting to do so or leaving it off intentionally at the time of slaughter rendered the sacrifice void and thus the meat forbidden for consumption. They also agree that **if other than God's name is mentioned then this would be forbidden**, due to the verse "Eat not of that (meat) on which Allah's Name has not been pronounced"* [Al-Anaam 6:121; emphasis added].[20]

*"Forbidden for you are carrion, and blood, and flesh of swine, and that which has been slaughtered **while proclaiming the name of any other than God**, and one killed by strangling, and one killed with blunt weapons, and one which died by falling, and that which was gored by the horns of some animal, and one eaten by a wild beast, except those whom you slaughter; and that which is slaughtered at the altar and*

---

[20] http://en.wikipedia.org/wiki/Dhabihah (11/21/11)

*that which is distributed by the throwing of arrows [for an omen]; **this is an act of sin**.*" (Al-Maa'idah 5:3; emphasis added)

So basically, the turkeys that we as a family have eaten for years during our Thanksgiving feasts are now off-limits because the birds are now being dedicated to a *false god*, which is really no God at all. Paul tells Christians that it is fine to eat meat that has been sacrificed to idols *if we are not aware of it*, but he also makes it clear that if we *know* food has been sacrificed to idols, we are to avoid eating it (cf. 1 Corinthians 8).

When it boils right down to it, the bottom line is that this continual *catering* to Islam has *got* to stop. While Butterball and other corporations are busy catering to Islam, they are forcing *me* and many others to go somewhere else for their turkeys. This makes no sense at all and is certainly not good business sense.

I do *not* like to *knowingly* eat meat sacrificed to *idols* and I will *not* do it. I am not going to eat meat that has been dedicated to Allah, because as far as I am concerned, Allah and the God of the Bible are not the same Person. If that is the case, then Allah can be only one individual: *Satan*.

This whole situation is ridiculous.

Part of the problem is also seen in how people respond to the protests by Christians regarding the halal-compliant turkeys. On their social networking page, Butterball had many complaints posted by people who were upset – and rightly so – that a food company would simply alter its product preparation procedures to suit one group.

Among the many complaints were posts directed toward Christians who were quickly seen as hate-mongering bigots. The point of the situation is completely lost on people like this. One woman posted that she was so happy that Butterball was now offering turkeys for "all faiths." I pointed out to her that this was inaccurate. In effect,

Butterball was now mainly offering their turkeys to Muslims. Orthodox Jews were no longer able to eat them, as well as other groups. I also made it clear that eating a Butterball halal-compliant turkey did not make me a Muslim, as one woman opined. The reality, though, is now that I know the turkeys coming from Butterball plants *have* been dedicated to a false idol/god, then to eat them would present a moral dilemma for the unsaved. That is Paul's point in 1 Corinthians 8. Christians should abstain from eating meat sacrificed to idols so that the unsaved or weaker brother does not stumble.

Yet, there are those who also posted on the Butterball social network page who quoted Jesus when He said that what goes into a person does not make them unclean. They also pointed to the situation in Acts where Peter is told to eat of any animal on the sheet that came down from heaven.

While both of those points are absolutely true, the reality is that love should always motivate me and while it is fine for me to eat anything, love should constrain me if it will cause someone to stumble. It's really that simple.

"To be halal certified the animal must be facing Mecca, have its throat cut while still alive and then ritually sacrificed by a Muslim who recites a prayer dedicating the slaughter to Allah. Fees must be paid to one of the certifying organisations (sic) for this service. Islamic certifying organisations (sic) benefit financially from providing this service. They receive a constant stream of funds to support Islamic projects which contribute to the advancement of sharia (Islamic law) here and around the world."[21]

The quote above from the source listed below also lists products that are now halal-compliant.[22] That is some list, and obviously, many of the products on that list were not "alive" as turkeys are alive, yet it is

---

[21] http://www.halalchoices.com.au/what_is_halal.html (11/22/11)
[22] http://www.halalchoices.com.au/product_lists_halal.html (11/22/11)

clear that even though there was no need to slaughter anything for a candy bar, there would still be a prayer dedicating the product to Allah, as explained in the quoted paragraph above.

If a Muslim wants his turkey to be halal-compliant, then he should go buy his own live turkey and have it done his way. They could also open their own poultry stores where halal-compliant chickens, turkeys, and other things could be purchased specifically for them. We do *not* need corporations to start slaughtering animals while some Imam (Islamic cleric) calls out the name of Allah during the process. After decades of eating Butterballs, Butterball has just lost me as a customer until and/or if this situation is ever corrected.

This is one of the big problems with Islam. Since Islam's entire ideology consumes the lives of the orthodox Muslim – *politically*, *religiously*, and *militarily* – it is impossible for a Muslim to separate one thing from another. In order for them to function *outside* of their own culture, the world is expected to *bend* to Islam. If not, they become upset, angry, and even murderous. The reader will recall the five-phase plan previously listed in this book.

So think of it. Muslims want to eat turkeys but they can't eat turkeys because the turkeys they want to eat are not halal-compliant. I can understand that and I can also sympathize with them. But the problem begins when they go to the turkey producers and simply "ask" them to make the turkeys halal-compliant, which involves the process previously cited and the calling out to Allah.

In the process of agreeing to make Butterball turkeys halal-compliant, they *must* include the ceremony previously described or the turkey does not become halal-compliant. So while Butterball Corp is worrying about ensuring that Muslims can eat their turkeys, they opt to go through the ceremonial process called Dhabihah, which includes dedicating that bird to Allah. Now that I am aware of this, I simply cannot eat that turkey, so Butterball has lost my business.

But there is a much larger problem here than simply Muslims wanting to have turkeys killed in a specific way and blessed by an Imam who calls on the name of Allah. More important than that is to understand what Muslims are doing to American society, just as they've done in other societies.

People need to realize that this is exactly how Muslims act in an open and free society. They do whatever they can to push themselves and their beliefs on city councils, corporations, colleges, and schools so that special privileges will be extended to them.

As a Christian, if I was in a courtroom and decided that it was time to say my prayers and proceeded to do so, as soon as the bailiffs realized what was going on, I would be escorted out. However, because Muslims are seen as coming from "third world" or otherwise underdeveloped nations where they still act like it is A.D. 600-700, they can't be expected to understand. After all, it's only their particular culture, so give them space to say their prayers. That's the mindset. But is that all it is, Muslims who should be extended privileges because they do not "understand" modern culture?

Muslim students attending a Roman Catholic College went to the administration asking the school to provide them with a room that is completely free of religious icons and imagery. What? It's a *Catholic* college.

Why on earth did they voluntarily decide to attend a Roman Catholic college if they are Muslims? The official word is that they "feel safer" there than at secular colleges. That is extremely difficult to believe. How often do we hear of crimes against Muslims in the U.S. solely because they are Muslim? You can bet if it existed, the liberal talking heads of the television news domain would be the first ones to bring it to the world.

In actuality, this move by these Muslim students is nothing but a ruse – a clever ruse – designed to allow Muslims to get what they want. Once they are given a room that is completely free of religious icons and imagery, they will ask for more. Then, they will need special ceremonial wash basins. Then they will need something else. Soon, they will literally be claiming areas of that Roman Catholic college for Allah without having to lift a sword.

This is what Islam is attempting to accomplish here in America. I'm sure the pundits and sympathizers of Islam will think that I'm simply going off and there is little intelligence to my words. That doesn't matter. Some of the things Islamic groups like CAIR are attempting to do right now in America are completely ridiculous, and yet they are moving forward because there are very few people standing in their way.

I would like to clearly state that Muslims are *welcome* in America *if* they come here through legal channels. They are *not* welcome to arrive and then quietly begin turning American society into an Islamic state based on their specific food needs or something else, yet this is what is happening. We are told (or it is implied) that in order for them to be part of society, America must give them what they want and "need." That's simply not true, but it allows them to conquer by working their beliefs through society.

No one is giving me what I want because of my Christianity, and I don't expect my government to stop using my tax dollars to pay for abortions any time soon. I don't expect the liberals in Congress to stop throwing my tax dollars away on asinine things. I don't expect those same liberals to all of a sudden do an about-face with respect to illegal aliens flooding into this country.

Corporations of America need to wake up! They cannot expect to be able to cater to *all* people. It's impossible. If Butterball had refused to make their turkeys halal-compliant, they would have lost *some* Muslim customers. Now that they have decided that Muslims are the only people they care to cater to, they have lost my business and many others are falling in line with me.

The truth is that Butterball could have set a number of birds aside and dedicated them to Islam. This would have left plenty of non-Islamic birds (for the lack of a better phrase) for the rest of us. There *should* be a choice, but Islam does not want people to have a choice. Islam intends to rule through acquisition. Once they begin to gain things for themselves, they continue on that path until they get more and more, and it then becomes too difficult for the rest of us to turn things around.

This almost occurred in The Netherlands because of their "hate-speech" laws that made it illegal to even comment on Islam, even if the comments were completely *true*. There is something despotic about that situation and it should not exist, but Islam is forcing the issue.

We are seeing the true nature of Islam, but *most* are still blind to it. Most people in this country probably don't care if a turkey is dedicated to Allah or not. They'll still eat it. These are the same people who do not believe that our country was founded on Christian principles (it was *not* founded as a Christian nation, but on Christian principles, and there is a difference) nor the real reason for Thanksgiving.

So which other companies and corporations are going to go halal-compliant? Which other corporations are going to see dollar signs with respect to Islam? What companies will begin to feel the pressure from Islamic groups that tells them they need to start catering to the people of Islam? What these companies need to realize is that they are making a decision to push certain groups of customers away, even while they attempt to attract others.

The most asinine thing about this whole situation is that for the orthodox Muslim, the time of Thanksgiving in America has no real meaning. They don't care about the Thanksgiving celebration that occurs in America! They are not interested in participating because they are grateful that America exists and they can immigrate to this country. In fact, these same orthodox Muslims see America as "the great Satan."

We'll see how this turns out, but until it changes – IF it changes – another producer of turkeys will get my business. That's just the way it is…

Chapter 9
Unequal Protection

Apparently, it's not good enough that Muslims are now asking for and receiving special privileges like turkeys that are halal-compliant. The worst part of what is happening in our country is that Muslims seem to be the only ideological group that *is* given special privileges, in spite of the U.S. Constitution.

However, when it comes to the rights of Christians, no such privileges seem to exist at all. In fact, in many situations, Christians are denied their rights under the guise of separation of church and state.

Such was the case of a young boy named Brian, a special needs student (he suffers from cerebral palsy) who was told in no uncertain terms that he was not allowed to dance to a song about Jesus in an upcoming talent show at his school. Brian did not understand what the problem was and it affected him as well as his parents.

Brian's mother Adrianna was told the following by the school's principal: *"This song says 'Jesus' too many times. Doesn't he have another he can dance to?"*[23] As Brian's mother explained to the principal, she could listen to his iPod and would learn that every song Brian listened to was about Jesus.

As Adrianna would soon learn, the principal of Superior Street Elementary School in Chatsworth, CA would lay down the law. According to the article, *"the principal was adamant: without a non-Christian song, Brian wouldn't take part in the show. Adriana hung up and started doing her homework."*[24]

Eventually, Arianna took their situation to the Alliance Defense Fund (ADF) after calling a local Christian radio station to determine whether or not her son Brian had the right to perform the song. After all, Brian had tried out for the talent show and had been chosen based on his performance, during which he had danced to that particular song that the principal said had too many references to Jesus in it.

A call to ADF helped Arianna understand that the school could *not* tell Brian that the song was not permissible. *"ADF attorneys saw the possibility that a lawsuit could impact millions of children like Brian all over the country. Because Brian was far from the only student being told he couldn't talk or sing or dance to a song about Jesus.*

---

[23] http://www.alliancedefensefund.org/TruthandTriumph/4-3/CoverStory (11/22/11)
[24] Ibid

"'Unfortunately, it is all too common,' says David Cortman, ADF Senior Counsel, who encouraged the Hickmans to file the lawsuit. 'Not only do you get the same situation – where the school denies [students' right to perform Christian songs] based on flat-out hostility or the so-called separation of church and state – but students are being censored from sharing their faith, wearing a religious T-shirt, starting Bible or pro-life clubs.'"[25]

It is clear that too many people misunderstand and misuse the separation of church and state clause in the founding documents of the United States. In this particular case, the school was not *forcing* students or a student to participate in a religious exercise. Brian is a Christian and as such, can talk about Jesus if he wants to *at school*.

In effect, the students wind up being *"told by their teacher, their principal, and their administrators that sharing your faith or merely mentioning Jesus, as in this case, is illegal, that you cannot do it in the public school."*[26] This is, of course, ridiculous, but this is also what the average person believes. The principal at Superior Street Elementary is obviously no different from most people.

The problem with the situation is that ADF had roughly one week to accomplish something for Brian, and that time crunch would make it very difficult. First, they filed a lawsuit. *"[The lawyer from ADF] and his team immediately set about personally serving the principal, the superintendent, and every member of the school board with a copy of the lawsuit. Days passed, with no response."*[27]

With only a few days left, the legal team tried another route. *"ADF attorneys resorted to Plan B: filing an emergency motion for a temporary restraining order to allow Brian to perform. Again, [ADF's legal] team personally served all the major defendants. This time, they ca-*

---

[25] http://www.alliancedefensefund.org/TruthandTriumph/4-3/CoverStory (11/22/11)
[26] Ibid
[27] Ibid

pitulated."[28] How does this happen in the United States of America? How do we go from being a country established on Christian principles to one in which there can be nothing that even *smacks* of religion in public places?

It happens because people do not understand the law. Those who do understand it may hope that people will not sue because of the money involved.

Let me provide a hypothetical example. Company A makes airbrushes and they are a very large company. Company B also makes airbrushes and they are much smaller in size. Company A decides that Company B took an idea they were going to use for a new line of airbrushes. Company B denies the charge. Company A sues. Company B heads to court. Soon, however, Company B realizes that it cannot continue to funnel as much money as they've been funneling into fighting the charges, and Company A shows no sign of letting up. The result? Company B gives up and essentially loses its company to Company A.

In this case, we have no idea which company was telling the truth and the courts never got a chance to decide. Company B simply ran out of money to continue the fight and because of it wound up giving everything up to Company A.

The Chatsworth School District is very large. They have a good amount of resources at their disposal and, like most large school districts, keep a legal team on retainer. The Hickman's are not rich, so fortunately for them, ADF took the case pro bono. All Adrianna wanted was an answer concerning her son's rights to dance to a song that happened to be about Jesus.

ADF wanted to take the case because it could ultimately benefit many young boys and girls who would find themselves in that same situa-

---

[28] http://www.alliancedefensefund.org/TruthandTriumph/4-3/CoverStory (11/22/11)

tion. In this case, a young Christian boy whose love for Jesus seems to know no bounds was at first denied his right of free speech by a principal who had no clue about what was admissible and what was not. Hopefully she understands now.

But what about other Christians across America and the world who are being told that they cannot do this or say that? Pakistan just announced that it is now forbidden to use the name "Jesus" in texting conversations between cell phone users. One might wonder how the authorities in Pakistan would know, but considering these countries have the ability to completely shut down the Internet or the ability to use cell phones, it is not too difficult to imagine that setting up some filter to track the use of the word "Jesus" could easily be done.

All of this leads us to ask *why even saying the Name of Jesus* is becoming something that people feel is best left out of the conversation. What is it about Jesus that people either come to love or hate?

Chapter 10
All-American Muslim?

In the never-ending process of Islam's attempt to bamboozle the public by presenting as much propaganda as possible through as many venues as possible, one of the latest sources of this propaganda comes to us in the form of a television show.

The TLC network has decided that Americans don't know enough about the true nature of Islam, so they came to the rescue to set the record straight, educating us along the way. The show *All-American*

Muslim follows the lives of a number of Muslim families and couples. We see laughing, sharing, eating, good-natured kidding and essentially everything we would see with any other well-rounded family or couple, and it all takes place in Dearborn, MI.

In case you're not aware, Dearborn, MI has become home to many Muslims. According to the U.S. Census Bureau report of 2010, the total population of Dearborn at that time was 4,779,736. Out of that, 3,275,394 were reported as "white," and interestingly enough, Arabs – for some strange reason – were included in this category.

Michigan has been known as the Muslim capitol of the U.S. for a number of years (going back to at least 2007).[29] Dearborn is the tenth most populated city in Michigan with respect to the number of Muslims who live there.

Back in 2009, another city in Michigan – Hamtramck – wound up with a city council in which half of the seats were taken by Muslims in spite of the fact that Muslims then made up only a third of the city's entire population. Unfortunately for Hamtramck – a city that was at one time largely Polish – the effects of militant Islamic incursion have divided the town.

Just one example is the fact that though city council members *have said* they want to unite people, the reality is that something else is happening. Regarding the issue of daily prayers, when "*hundreds of long-time residents of Hamtramck, MI protested the city allowing the five-times-per-day Muslim call to prayer to be broadcast over Hamtramck's loudspeakers, the city council voted unanimously in April 2004 to allow it.*"[30]

This is a terrible precedent, largely because it disallowed due process and the involvement of the non-Muslim tax payers. The city council

---

[29] http://www.renewamerica.com/columns/zieve/070111
[30] Ibid

allotted no time for non-Muslim residents to address the city council, essentially blocking the democratic process that is guaranteed under the U.S. Constitution.

"[R]esident Bob Golen was outraged by the city council's actions and said: 'So they had made up their mind before any public meeting and it's been five-nothing ever since. This is only the beginning. They're going to use Hamtramck as a precedent. This is coming to your town, to the town down the road, and to the [next] town down the road.' Golen added that, after the city council voted to allow the calls to prayer, one of the city councilmen said that he was 'proud to set a precedent in this country'."[31]

It seems clear that what the city council would prefer is if everyone and anyone who had a problem with their decision simply *leave*. While they do not say that, it is certainly implied in their decision to ignore a large portion of the populace in Hamtramck. One wonders how a city council can get away with something like this, but there again it is likely that the Muslims on the council have taken advantage of every loophole available to them. If this does not represent the intrusion of Sharia Law into a community, what does?

Apparently, average Muslims are not the only kind living in Michigan, which has also become home to aspects of Hezbollah. *"Terrorist Hezbollah is also firmly established in Michigan and in 2006 the owner of the La Shish chain of 15 US restaurants, Talal Chahine, fled to Lebanon rather than facing federal charges that he had both evaded paying taxes and funneled $20 million in profits to Hezbollah. This is but one case and there is little doubt other terrorist-supporting activities continue to occur right under our radar. Dearborn's Al Mabarat 'charitable organization' has also been named in providing funds to Hezbollah*

---

[31] http://www.renewamerica.com/columns/zieve/070111

and on 31 July 3,500 Dearborn Muslims marched in support of Hezbollah and shouted: 'Jews are diseased!'"[32]

As if that isn't enough, it also appears that numerous other allegedly criminal or terrorist groups live, work, and play in Michigan. *"Hezbollah is not the only Islamic terrorist organization that has a stronghold in Michigan. Terrorist groups al-Qaeda, Hamas, the Muslim Brotherhood and al-Gama'at al-Islamiyya are also firmly entrenched in the state. And it is not only in Michigan that these terrorists have gained a foothold — their presence is now spread throughout the US. We continue to allow the presence of those within our country who have stated and are bent upon overthrowing and destroying it. Too many tolerance-advocates continue to act in an insane and self-destructive manner by allowing these incursions to exist — placing the rest of us not only at risk but, at the mercy of our destructors. And it is now happening not only on our soil but, in our backyards."*[33]

So with all this happening, why is TLC trying to show us how "normal" Muslims look, act, and live in Michigan? One would surmise that the only reason is due to pressure to propagandize the situation in Michigan that much further. It is likely hoped that those who watch the program will feel less inclined to stereotype Muslims as terrorists.

Unfortunately, for anyone who really cares to know, Michigan is not a place where non-Muslims might feel comfortable. If terrorists have been located there and if certain city councils are railroading their pet projects through to the disdain of most residents, then what does that say about what Islam is attempting to do in areas like this?

---

[32] http://www.renewamerica.com/columns/zieve/070111
[33] Ibid

Chapter 11

Is Mr. Obama a Muslim?

The question won't die. Of course, those who bring it up are made to look like idiots or morons, as evidenced by the individual I quoted a few chapters ago who asked, "*Or you part of the wacky morons that believe that he's a Muslim, or not an American?*"

This type of question is designed to make the individual who is tempted to believe that Mr. Obama is either not eligible to be president of the U.S. or that he is a Muslim (or both) look as if he has lost his marbles. What do you do with that? Well, fortunately, there are some individuals who can shed light onto the question of Mr. Obama's religious persuasion.

Usama Dakdok began The Straight Way of Grace Ministry in 2001. Born into a Christian home in Egypt, Usama became Christian himself. Yet because of his upbringing, he grew up alongside many Muslims, learned to read, write, and speak Arabic fluently, and understands what constitutes a Muslim.

On his website, he lists a variety of facts concerning Mr. Obama and why all of these facts point to his being a Muslim. The following is quoted from http://thestraightway.org/obama.asp:

1. *He was born from Muslim blood. (Which in Islam makes him automatically a Muslim).*
2. *He was educated in a school where as Muslim he was educated on Islam for a minimum of two hours weekly.*
3. *For a better education he attended a Catholic school, which many Muslims do.*
4. *He had nothing to do with Christianity until he married his wife.*
5. *He joined a cult church, a non-Christian church.*
    a. *The church teaches separatism (black and white)*
    b. *They teach black theology, not Christ Theology*
    c. *The church honors and respects Islam and Muslims to the point they welcome Muslims to be members of the church and gave Louis Farrakhan an award for being the man who will unite the true Christian to the true Muslim to the true Jew. WHAT A CHRISTIAN CHURCH!*
    d. *Why would Obama leave Islam to join such a church? He joined skillfully to cover-up, knowing that a Muslim in America would have little chance to become a senator or the president.*
    e. *When you believe in Mohammad you deny Christ.*

6. He never denounced Islam or Mohammad or the Qur'an.
7. There is no record that he was baptized.
8. From his own words, we can judge him, for he made fun of Christianity, the Bible, Old Testament and New Testament, which proves he is not a Christian.
9. When a Muslim leaves Islam to Christianity, there would be a 100% fatwa (decree for him to be killed) issued against his life.
    a. A Fatwa has never been issued on Obama. But the opposite is true, for the Muslim world is endorsing and supporting him. This includes Louis Farrakhan's endorsement. Some may say that Obama has distanced himself for his radical minister and from Louis Farrakhan but my response is very simple, it is an act because he, his pastor, and Farrakhan, know if he does not say that. He will lose the vote of the rest of the country.
    b. He was welcomed to Kenya as a Muslim hero recently
    c. Muslims in America support him, even financially "One dollar for one nation under God "(Allah).
    d. As a senator, he has and continues to employ members of The Nation of Islam. Cynthia K. Miller was the treasurer of His U.S. Senate campaign. Jennifer Mason is Obama's director of Constituent Services in his U.S. Senate office and is also in charge of selecting Obama's senate interns. - (debbieschlussel.com)
10. His agenda for the Whitehouse clearly shows he is Muslim.
    a. Remove our army immediately from the Middle East.
    b. He sits and eats dinner with Muslim jihadist.
    c. Removing the idea of the use of nuclear weapons in any circumstance.
    d. Passing a hate crime bill that will silence anyone who speaks against Islam.

11. *His stance on the issue of gay marriage and abortion proves he is not a Christian.*

In truth, according to what is stated above, it would certainly appear as though Mr. Obama is indeed a Muslim. Many might ask, *so what?* Isn't it bigotry to say that a Muslim cannot be president of the United States? The problem is far more difficult than that.

It is not simply that a Muslim is a president of the United States. What is bothersome is what Mr. Obama has done since *becoming* president with all of his deference to Islam. This is a serious situation because much of Islam (if not all of it) wants to see America destroyed.

If Mr. Obama is a Muslim, then the chances are great that he does not have this country's best interest at heart. He is serving as president, but very possibly with an ulterior motive to help bring down this country from within by making life palatable for Muslims living in this country by enabling them to gain favors from the administration through legislation.

In the quote above, note the items listed in item number ten, specifically 10d. Why would any president of the United States (or of any nation) try to pass legislation that would essentially offer protection to one specific group of people, a group that is essentially *religious* in nature?

It is reminiscent of what Constantine laid the groundwork for that enabled Christianity to become married to the state in the fourth century A.D. In essence, Constantine made Christianity acceptable throughout the Roman Empire. Prior to him becoming emperor, Christians were heavily persecuted. When Constantine essentially "okay'd" Christianity, persecution went out the door almost immediately.

With Mr. Obama's efforts in attempting to "okay" Islam, it will become a crime to speak in negative terms regarding Islam, even if what is spoken is true. The truthfulness of the statement will not matter.

The world has already witnessed this occurring in the United Kingdom, where people are routinely arrested and tossed in jail for making statements that wind up offending Muslims in that country. Great Britain is not the only country where this happens, either.

There is something drastically wrong when legislation must be passed to ensure that people will not speak their minds about a particular group of people. This is the way Islam works, though. Islam endeavors to remove freedom of speech, effectively placing a gag over the mouths of individuals who are trying to educate people as to the problems of Islam. However, this is not tolerated.

Notice that Christianity receives no such privilege. People are free to say whatever they want to say against Christianity and can and do use the Name of Jesus as a swear word whenever it suits them. But say that Muhammad married a nine-year old girl and there could very well be hell to pay. It's fine if a Muslim says it, but don't let them hear a non-Muslim (or "infidel") say it. Truth is truth and it should not matter who says it.

Chapter 12
Bridging the Gap?

The more we read of Islam and radical Muslims, the more difficult it is to let our guard down. However, one particular church in the western part of the United States has managed to not only lower its guard but participate in numerous activities that are designed to desensitize people to the problems that are inherent within Islam.

I'm referring – unfortunately – to Rick Warren's Saddleback Church. Of late, Rick has tried reaching out to the Muslim community, and let me say at the outset that there is nothing wrong with this at all. Christians *should* reach out to everyone, including Muslims. They should do so because all people need Jesus and the salvation that He offers. Salvation comes from no other.

So what's the problem then? Well, put simply, it appears as though the folks at Saddleback under the leadership of Mr. Warren are actually coming together in a form of a blended group, as opposed to preaching the gospel to the Muslims.

According to one news source, Warren *"has embarked on an effort to heal divisions between evangelical Christians and Muslims by partnering with Southern California mosques and proposing a set of theological principles that includes acknowledging that Christians and Muslims worship the same God."*[34] The first question to ask is how can anyone think that Christians and Muslims worship the same God? If both groups worship the same God, then someone does not have salvation. I say that because of the theological beliefs of Christians as opposed to those of Muslims. The beliefs are not at all the same.

In fact, if one boils it down, it becomes clear that Islam is primarily a works-based religion, not unlike many other religious systems that rely heavily on what a person *does* or does *not* do as the determining factor in inheriting eternal life.

Much of Islam appears to have more in common with the ancient Egyptian religions than with Christianity. Yet, here we have Warren's Saddleback Church involved in outreach with Muslims not by stating the gospel, but by affirming that both groups worship the same God.

"The effort, informally dubbed King's Way, caps years of outreach between Warren and Muslims. Warren has broken Ramadan fasts at a

---

[34] http://www.ocregister.com/articles/muslims-341669-warren-saddleback.html (2/27/2012)

Mission Viejo mosque, met Muslim leaders abroad and addressed 8,000 Muslims at a national convention in Washington D.C."[35] There is, unfortunately, something very wrong and even dangerous about this approach.

It would be like a Christian and a Mormon sitting down together and determining that though there are theological differences, we worship the same God; therefore, we are brothers in Christ. This is an untenable position, yet it is one that Rick Warren seems intent on pushing.

I'm *not* saying that we should not reach out to the Muslim community. Actually, we should reach out to all religious systems that stand juxtaposed against Christianity because of their particular doctrinal slant.

There is nothing wrong with getting together and enjoying the company of Muslims. Warren's church has set up soccer games in which Christian leaders and Muslim imams play against Christian and Muslim teens. Is there anything wrong with that? No, there isn't.

The only problem that truly exists is when Christianity is compared with Islam and the two are found to be *similar* because of the God that is supposedly shared by the two.

Let's look at this another way. The modern Jew is lost without Jesus. If anyone worships the same God as the Christian, it would have to be the Jew, not the Muslim. Yet, in spite of that, the modern Jew (and we are not talking about Messianic Jews) fails to understand that Jesus is the way, the truth, and the life. Jesus came as the Messiah to the nation of Israel and was roundly rejected.

---

[35] http://www.ocregister.com/articles/muslims-341669-warren-saddleback.html (2/27/2012)

Since Jesus is God, it is clear that the Jews who reject Jesus reject God, though they believe they are worshiping the One, true God (if they are orthodox Jews).

As Paul tells us in Romans 9-11, we owe a debt of gratitude to the Jews because it is from them that Jesus came and now offers salvation to a dying world.

It was not through Islam that Jesus came, but through Judaism. He Himself was Jewish regarding His humanity. He was also God in the flesh.

In effect then, Christianity has far more in common with Judaism than with Islam. If we consider the history of Islam, we note that it did not begin until Muhammad in the A.D. 600s. Judaism is far older than that and it is because of Abraham, Isaac, and Jacob that we have Christianity. Islam is an offshoot of Ishmael, and though his father was Abraham, that's as far as it goes.

The question that must be asked is why isn't Rick Warren doing the same type of reaching out to Jews as he is to Muslims? Why is Chrislam becoming such a big thing?

"Saddleback worshippers have invited Muslims to Christmas dinner and played interfaith soccer at a picnic in Irvine attended by more than 300 people. (The game pitted pastors and imams against teens from both faiths. The teens won.)

"The effort by a prominent Christian leader to bridge what polls show is a deep rift between Muslims and evangelical Christians culminated in December at a dinner at Saddleback attended by 300 Muslims and members of Saddleback's congregation.

"At the dinner, Abraham Meulenberg, a Saddleback pastor in charge of interfaith outreach, and Jihad Turk, director of religious affairs at a

mosque in Los Angeles, introduced King's Way as 'a path to end the 1,400 years of misunderstanding between Muslims and Christians'."[36]

I firmly believe that this effort on the part of Saddleback is fully misguided and misplaced. The reason there is "misunderstanding between Muslims and Christians" is due to the fact that, in spite of what Rick Warren may believe, Christians and Muslims do not worship the same God, and neither do Jews and Christians. We cannot bridge any gap by attempting to fellowship with Muslims.

The only way the gap is bridged is through the gospel of Jesus Christ. He is the One who bridges the gap.

One of the things that Saddleback has come up with is a document that seeks to compare the alleged similarities between Christianity and Islam. " *'We agreed we wouldn't try to evangelize each other,' said [Jihad] Turk. 'We'd witness to each other but it would be out of "Love Thy Neighbor," not focused on conversion'.*"[37]

That does not make sense. You cannot evangelize someone unless you are willing to show them where they are *wrong,* and I'd have to say that Saddleback has it wrong because of this errant approach.

How do you "witness to each other" without pointing out that we need Jesus because of the fact that all have sinned and fallen short? To witness to a Muslim means at some point showing that Muhammad is not the way, but Jesus is the way. This can and should be done lovingly, but nonetheless, it definitely needs to be done! It cannot be avoided, and by doing so we are guilty of not truly loving our neighbor.

Warren seems to be trying to create bridges made of sand. Does he ever get around to telling Muslims that they need Jesus? It does not

---

[36] http://www.ocregister.com/articles/muslims-341669-warren-saddleback.html (2/27/2012)
[37] Ibid

appear to be the case. In a speech to roughly 8,000 Muslims in Washington, DC, Warren told the group, *"I don't know if you have noticed this, but God likes variety."*[38]

Is that supposed to be one of those "gotcha" moments? Should we insert the "applause" sign here? Of *course* God loves variety, but there is only *one* way to Him and that is through Jesus Christ. It is not through Muhammad via Jesus. It is directly through Jesus.

The trouble is that I cannot help but wonder if Rick Warren is doing far more harm than good. Certainly, any Muslim imam would not take kindly to being told that Jesus is the only way to God. Moreover, they would do what they could to protect their Muslim flock from hearing that as well.

Why does it always seem as though it is Christianity that needs to be the system that compromises so that other people will feel more comfortable about themselves and their particular belief system? Why is Jesus the One who must always make exceptions to the rule that He Himself lived by and created?

One of the disheartening things that seems to be transpiring within these efforts to fellowship with Muslims is that downplaying of conversion. *"Gwynne Guibord, an ordained Episcopal priest and co-founder of a Los Angeles outreach group that fosters relationships between churches and mosques nationwide, said Saddleback's effort is unprecedented. 'I'm not aware of any other evangelical church reaching out to the Muslim community,' she said."*[39]

What Guibord calls outreach should probably be called fellowship. Ray Comfort and others have stated that "friendship evangelism" simply doesn't work, and I have found that to be the case as well.

---

[38] http://www.ocregister.com/articles/muslims-341669-warren-saddleback.html (2/27/2012)
[39] Ibid

People need to hear the gospel. Playing soccer or having dinner with people of opposing faiths is fine, but at some point, the gospel needs to be discussed.

Guibord continues, *""I think that many evangelicals feel a mandate to convert people to Christianity.'...Because the Consultative Group was founded to respond to increasing antagonism between the two faiths, 'we would not have made headway' if one side was trying to convert the other, she said. Now, she said, it might be possible to include evangelicals in her group's work."*[40]

Yes, I would wholeheartedly agree that evangelicals believe we have a mandate to convert people to Christianity. That's a given, but Guibord acts as if it's a mystery as to how people have arrived at that juncture. It's because of the Great Commission. Jesus *told* us to do that.

Unfortunately, those within the Episcopalian denomination are not noted for their willingness to evangelize the lost. Some certainly do, but as a denomination, it's not a top priority. Sadly, many denominations are like that.

Paul spent his adult life as a Christian preaching to lost groups of people. He didn't care who they were; he wanted them saved. Even when he preached on Mars Hill, his jumping off point was the "unknown god" that they worshiped. Paul did not take the time to develop relationships with people. He was far more interested in getting the salvation message out to the lost person. The lost person is anyone who does not know Jesus as Savior and Lord.

Muslims qualify as lost people. On one hand, Rick Warren is doing a great thing by opening his heart to the people of Islam. He supports them. He buys candy and magazine subscriptions from their chil-

---

[40] http://www.ocregister.com/articles/muslims-341669-warren-saddleback.html (2/27/2012)

dren. He invites them to dinner and joins them for dinner. This is all well and good because he is showing them that he loves them.

However, if we truly love people, we will want them to be *saved* from eternal death. Look at Acts chapter eight. There we read about Philip, who was directed by the Holy Spirit to preach to an Ethiopian eunuch. Philip did not take the time to befriend the man. He didn't invite him to his home for dinner. He preached the gospel. Because of that, the eunuch became saved that very day.

When we look over Jesus' life or the lives of His apostles, we see that Jesus was far more concerned with salvation for the lost than anything else. Yes, He ate dinner with people. Yes, he sat with people at a well. But He preached the gospel to them. He did not allow them to leave without hearing the gospel message.

When Jesus went to Zacheus' house, yes, he went there to eat, but He also went there to ensure that Zacheus had received salvation. Jesus did not mince words. He was clear and direct, whether He was talking to Zacheus or Nicodemus.

Why have we gotten to a point of believing that it is more profitable to do what Jesus did not do? We need to preach the gospel to everyone, including Muslims. We need to do it today.

Chapter 14

The End?

"For all have sinned, and come short of the glory of God." – Romans 3:23

Do you know *when* you will die? Are you aware of the *day* and *hour* when you will slip from this life into eternity? I'm betting you are not privy to that information. So why are you living as if you **_do_** know when it will happen? Putting a decision about Jesus off until another day is taking a huge chance because of the fact that you do not know when you will die. That is plainly simple, and logic alone demands that you do not put this decision off. Yet you do, because the thought of becoming a Christian makes you feel uncomfortable.

You wrongly believe that to become a Christian means that you have to change in a major way *before* Jesus will accept you. It means to you giving up the things you love now because if you love them, then obviously they are wrong and God does not love them.

You are putting the cart before the horse. You must understand that God is not rejecting you. He is not standing there, tapping His foot, demanding that you eliminate those things that He does not like before you can come to Him for salvation.

If you (or anyone) could do that, you would not *need* His salvation at all. It is because you and I do things that are not pleasing to Him that we need His salvation.

What do you do that you would like to no longer do? Do you drink excessively until you cannot control it? Do you play around with drugs? Do you eat too much food until you have become overweight, lethargic and sickly?

What other things are in your life that you do not like? Are you drawn to illicit extra-marital affairs? Do you have a problem with lust? Are you a shopaholic? Do you tend to tell lies a great deal because it makes you feel important, or to hide things about your life?

Do you find that you do not like people and you would prefer to be around animals or out in the woods than around people? Are you a workaholic? Do you place a high value on money and you find that you work very hard to obtain it?

Here's the problem. The enemy of our souls comes to us and tells us that God will never accept us until we get rid of those things. He lies to us that God essentially wants us "perfect" before He will be willing to meet us and grant us eternal life. This is completely untrue.

The other lie that our enemy tells us is that we should not become a Christian because the fun in our life will fly out the door. We will no longer be able to drink or do the fun things we enjoy now. We start to think that coming to God means becoming a doormat for people and having to fill our life with things we do not want to *ever* do.

These are all lies, and unfortunately, too many people believe them. First of all, God does not expect you to be "perfect" before you come to Him for salvation. If that were the case, no one would be able to ever approach Him.

Secondly, God does not say that He is going to take away all the things we enjoy and replace them with things we hate. What is wrong with enjoying the lake on your boat? What is wrong with spending a day with the family fishing or just relaxing in the mountains? There is nothing wrong with these things.

What God *will* do is begin to remove the things that have ensnared you so that life is actually draining from you, but you are not aware of it. For instance, maybe you drink excessively and you have tried everything you can think of to quit. You have gone to AA meetings, spent thousands of dollars on this program or that, and you have even used your own will power to free yourself from the addiction to alcohol, all to no avail.

The question is not: *do I need to quit before I come to Jesus?* The question is: *am I willing to allow Him to work in and through me to take away the addiction I have to alcohol?* Do you see the difference? Are you willing to allow Him to work in you to break that addiction so that you will become a healthier person, one who is able to think straight and one who learns to rely on Him for strength? That is all He wants you to be able to do. He knows you cannot break that addiction (or any addiction for that matter) with your own strength and willpower. Are you willing to allow Him to do it in and through you?

What if you are a workaholic? What if you have "things" like a boat, a house in Cancun, a large bank account, four cars, and more? Do you think that God is going to ask you to give it up, or worse, do you think that God will simply come in and take all of that from you? I know of nothing in Scripture that tells us He will do that.

What God will do with all of those who come to Him trusting Him for salvation is one thing, which begins the moment we receive salvation and will continue until the day we stand before Him. He will begin to create within us the character of Jesus (cf. Ephesians 2:10).

Here is a verse from the Old Testament that was said originally through the prophet Ezekiel to the people of Israel. While this was specifically stated to the Jews, it is applicable to all who receive salvation through Jesus Christ.

"I will give you a new heart and put a new spirit within you; I will take the heart of stone out of your flesh and give you a heart of flesh. I will put My Spirit within you and cause you to walk in My statutes and you will keep My judgments and do them" (Ezekiel 36:26-27).

God is speaking here through Ezekiel, and He is saying that He will give the people a new heart of flesh, removing that old heart of stone. This is God's responsibility. God is the One who makes that happen. We are told in the book of Hebrews that God is the Author and Finisher of our faith (cf. Hebrews 12:2). This tells me that God is the One who changes me from within so that over time, my desires are slowly turned into His desires.

I recall years ago thinking that God wanted to do everything in my life that I did not want Him to do. I fell into the asinine belief that He wanted to change everything about me. What I learned is that yes, there are things that God does want to change about me. However, there is a lot that God originally gave me that He has also enhanced and used for His glory.

Maybe you are a workaholic who thinks that working hard is something God does not want you to do. This is not necessarily the case. He may have given you the ability and the knowledge to work in the area of finance for a great purpose. All He may wind up doing is dialing back your workaholic tendencies so that you have more time to enjoy your family and study His Word.

But you say you smoke, or drink, or use illegal drugs, and you don't want to give those up. As I stated, you can't give those up under your own power, and the fact that you have tried so many times has proven it to you.

But God knows what is and what is not good for you. Are you willing to *allow* Him to work in you to change your desires so that you no longer want to smoke, use illegal drugs, or drink nearly as much?

Then you say that you believe God wants to make you a Christian so you can become miserable. Isn't that what most Christians are – miserable? Not the Christians I know, and certainly not me, my wife, or our children.

Where does the Bible say that God wants us miserable? You will not find it. What God wants is for us to be blessed, and that begins when we receive salvation from His hand.

You know if we would stop and take the time to consider the fact that this life is exceedingly short if we compare it to eternity, we will then realize that there is nothing so important that it should keep us from receiving Jesus as Savior and Lord.

Unfortunately, too many people do not consider the brevity of life. They think they will live forever, or at the very least, they will die when they are really old and gray. That will come too soon. Even though I have just recently turned 54, it still truly seems like yesterday that I was a young boy fishing in the Delaware River near Hobart, New York. There I spent many Saturdays fishing and simply enjoying being outdoors. How did life go by so very quickly? How could that have happened?

It has happened, and I am at a point in life where not only do I realize that this life is short, but I actually look forward to spending eternity with Jesus after this life. Does that sound morbid to you? It shouldn't, because by comparing this life to eternity, we should get a sense of what is truly important.

God does not expect us to become Mother Theresas. He does not necessarily expect us to give up everything and become missionaries in outer Mongolia. What God expects is for us to simply allow Him to change our character as He sees fit.

Over time, we may well find that we have simply stopped swearing without realizing it. Our desire for cigarettes or alcohol has nearly evaporated. Illicit affairs no longer enter the picture.

We also may find that some of the things we want to eliminate in our life become more pronounced. Often the enemy will do this to cause us to focus on something that God is not even doing in our lives at that point. It causes tension, frustration, and self-anger.

If you have gotten to this point in your life and you have not dealt with the question about Jesus, it is about time you do so. You need to stop what you are doing and realize a couple of things before you go through another minute in this life.

- **Sinner**: you need to realize that you are a sinner. You have sinned and you will continue to sin. Sin is breaking the laws that God has set up. We all sin. We have all broken God's laws and that breaks any connection we might have had with God. Sin pushes us away from Him.

   Romans 3:23 says, *"For all have sinned, and come short of the glory of God."* That means you and that means me. All means all. That is the first step. We need to recognize and agree with God that yes, we are sinners. I'm a sinner. You are a sinner. This results in God's anger, what the Bible terms "wrath."

- **God's Wrath**: Romans 1:18 says, *"For the wrath of God is revealed from heaven against all ungodliness and unrighteousness of men, who suppress the truth in unrighteousness."*

This is as much a fact as the truth that we are all sinners. Because we are sinners – by breaking God's law(s) – God has every right to be angry with us and ultimately destroy that which is sinful. If we choose to remain "in" our sinful states throughout this life, we will – unfortunately – be destroyed with the rest of sin.

Fortunately, there *is* a remedy, and it is salvation.

- **God's Gift**: In the sixteenth chapter of Acts, a jailer asks Paul this famous question: *what must I do to be saved?* The question was asked because Paul and Barnabas had been imprisoned, and while there, they began singing praises to God.

God then sent a powerful earthquake that opened the doors to all the prison cells, yet no one escaped. When the jailer arrived, he saw that everyone was still in their cells and after seeing that miracle (what prisoner would not want to escape from prison?), turned and asked what he must do to be saved. He was speaking of the spiritual aspect of things. He wanted to know how he could be guaranteed eternal life.

The answer Paul gave the man was, *"Believe on the Lord Jesus Christ, and thou shalt be saved, and thy house"* (Acts 16:31).

This is not head knowledge or intellectual assent. This is *believing from the heart*. In fact, Paul makes a very similar statement in another book he wrote, Romans. He says, *"That if thou shalt confess with thy mouth the Lord Jesus, and shalt believe in thine heart that God hath raised him from the dead, thou shalt be saved. For with the heart man believeth unto righteousness; and with the mouth confession is made unto salvation"* (Romans 10:9-10).

When we fully believe something, we confess that it is true. It must begin in the heart because that is where the will is located. We must want to believe. We must endeavor to believe. We must seek to believe.

We must stop giving ourselves all the reasons to deny or ignore Jesus. As God, He became a Man, born of a virgin. He clothed Himself with humanity that He might show us how to live, and in so doing, would keep every portion of the law.

If Jesus was capable of keeping every portion of the law, then He would be found worthy to become a sacrifice for our sin – yours and mine. If He became a sacrifice for our sin, then all that we must do is embrace Him and His sacrificial death.

In short then, to become saved we must:

1. Admit (we sin)
2. Repent (want to turn away from it)
3. Believe (that Jesus is the answer)
4. Embrace (the truth about Jesus)

We **admit** that we are sinner, that we have sinned. This is nothing more than agreeing with God that we have broken His law. Can you honestly say that you have not broken God's law? If you admit to breaking even the "smallest" law, then you are a lawbreaker.

After we admit that we have sinned, the next step is found in **repenting**. Some believe that repenting is actually moving away from sin. This author believes that it is a willingness to move away from sin, and there is a difference.

As we have already discussed, it is impossible to stop sinning. Human beings simply cannot do it because as long as we live, we will have a sin nature, which is something within us that gives us a propensity to sin. As long as we have this inner propensity to sin or break God's laws, we will never be perfect in this life.

We cannot one day say, "Lord, I promise to stop sinning." If we do that, we are only kidding ourselves and setting ourselves up for major failure. We cannot stop sinning in this life. The most we can do is *want* to stop sinning and then spend the rest of our lives allowing God to create the character of Jesus within us, slowly, little by little.

Repenting is to decide that you no longer want to do the things that keep us out of heaven. We no longer wish to break God's laws. It is not promising God that we will never sin again.

Once we admit, then repent, we must **believe**. This is one of the most difficult things to do because believing that Jesus died in our place, that He lived a perfectly sinless life, is extremely difficult to believe. Our minds cannot grasp that truth. We must ask God to open our eyes to that truth so that we can embrace it.

While on the cross next to Jesus, the one thief joined the other thief in ridiculing Jesus. Then, all of a sudden – as we read in Luke 23 – this same thief that had just been ridiculing Him now turned to Him with a new understanding.

It was this new understanding that prompted the thief to say to Jesus, *"Lord, remember me when you come into your Kingdom."* Jesus looked at the man and responded to him, *"Today, you will be with me in paradise."*

What had occurred in the mind and heart of that thief from one moment to the next? One thing, and that one thing was that God opened the thief's eyes so that he could see the truth. It was as if the blinders fell off and he now saw and understood who Jesus was, even to the most cursory degree that Jesus was dying not for Himself, but for others.

It was this understanding, this awareness, which prompted the man to ask Jesus to simply be remembered. Jesus went way beyond it to promise the man that he would be with Jesus that day in paradise.

Please notice in Luke 23 that there is nothing in the chapter that tells us that the man promised Jesus he would give up sin, or that he would never sin again. There is nothing that tells us that thief took the time to enter into a final deathbed confession of his sins so that he could be absolved.

The thief made no promises to Jesus at all. What he experienced was the truth of who Jesus was and what Jesus accomplished for humanity. Jesus accomplished what we cannot. What is left is for each person to *admit*, *repent*, *believe*, and *embrace*.

Let me clarify here that though we do not see any verbal repentance from the thief, we know that he did repent. He admitted as well. How can we know this? Simply due to the thief's complete about-face with respect to his attitude toward Jesus. One minute, he was ridiculing Jesus, and the next, embracing Him. This is important. There is no way he could have or would have *embraced* Jesus had he not been humbled by the truth *about* Jesus.

Once the thief saw the truth, he was instantly humbled. Within himself, he knew that he was a sinner, and in fact the text states that this is what he told the other thief dying next to him. *"But the other answering rebuked him, saying, Dost not thou fear God, seeing thou art in the same condemnation? And we indeed justly; for we receive the due reward of our deeds: but this man hath done nothing amiss"* (Luke 23:40-41). Something happened within the heart of the one thief. In one moment, the thief went from harassing Jesus to recognizing his own sinfulness, and then ultimately asking for grace, which was freely given to him.

Whether he said it or not, the thief went from haughtiness to humility in a very short space of time, and it was all because he saw the truth about Jesus. That truth helped him realize that he deserved his death and what would happen to him after death. He understood that Jesus did not deserve death.

From here, the thief fully embraced the truth about Jesus and was rewarded with eternal life because of it. He did not come off the cross to be water baptized. He did not list a long litany of offenses against God. He recognized the truth about Jesus, was humbled, and embraced that truth!

This is what each of us needs to do. We cannot give in to the lie that tells us that we are not good enough, or we have not given up enough before God will accept us. We must reject the lie that says we must somehow earn our salvation.

Jesus has done everything that is necessary to make salvation available to us. The only thing that is left for us is to see the truth. Once we see that truth, it should humble us to the point of embracing Jesus and all that He stands for and is to us.

The eighth chapter of Romans begins with the fact that all who trust Jesus for salvation are no longer condemned...*ever*. All of my sins – past, present, and future – have not only been forgiven, but canceled. It is because of my faith in the atonement (death) of Jesus that God is able to cancel all of my sins, even the ones that I have not committed yet. This does not make me eager to commit them. It makes me want to do what I can to avoid sinning.

If you do not know Jesus, please do not put down this book without deliberately *believing* that He is God, that He died for you by the shedding of His blood on the cross, and that He rose three days later because death could not keep Him. Do you believe that? If you do not yet believe it, do you *want* to believe it? If so, then simply ask God to help you come to believe all that Jesus is and all that He has accomplished for you. God will answer your prayers and you may either receive instantaneous awareness of all that Jesus is and has done, or it may be a *growing* awareness over time. In either case, it is the most important decision you will ever make.

Turn to Him now and pray for knowledge of the truth and an ability to embrace it. Please. He is waiting for you.

Ask Yourself:

1. Do you *know* Jesus? Are you in *relationship* with Him? Have you had a spiritual transaction according to John 3?
2. Do you *want* to receive eternal life through the only salvation that is available?
3. Do you believe that Jesus is God the Son, who was born of a virgin, lived a sinless life, died a bloody and gruesome death to pay for your sin, was buried, and rose again on the third day? Do you *believe* this?
4. Do you *want* to *embrace* the truth from #3?
5. Pray that God will open your eyes and provide you with the faith to begin believing the truth about Jesus. Ask Him to help your faith embrace the truth, realizing that you are not good enough to save yourself and that your sin will keep you out of God's Kingdom without His salvation.
6. Pray as if your life depended upon it because *it does*!
7. If you have prayed to receive Jesus as Savior and Lord, please write to me. I want to send you some materials at *no charge or obligation*. Write to me at **fred_deruvo@hotmail.com** and

sign up for our free bimonthly newsletter at
www.studygrowknow.com

Visit our page on **SermonAudio.com/study-grow-know** to hear our latest broadcasts as well as those that have been archived.

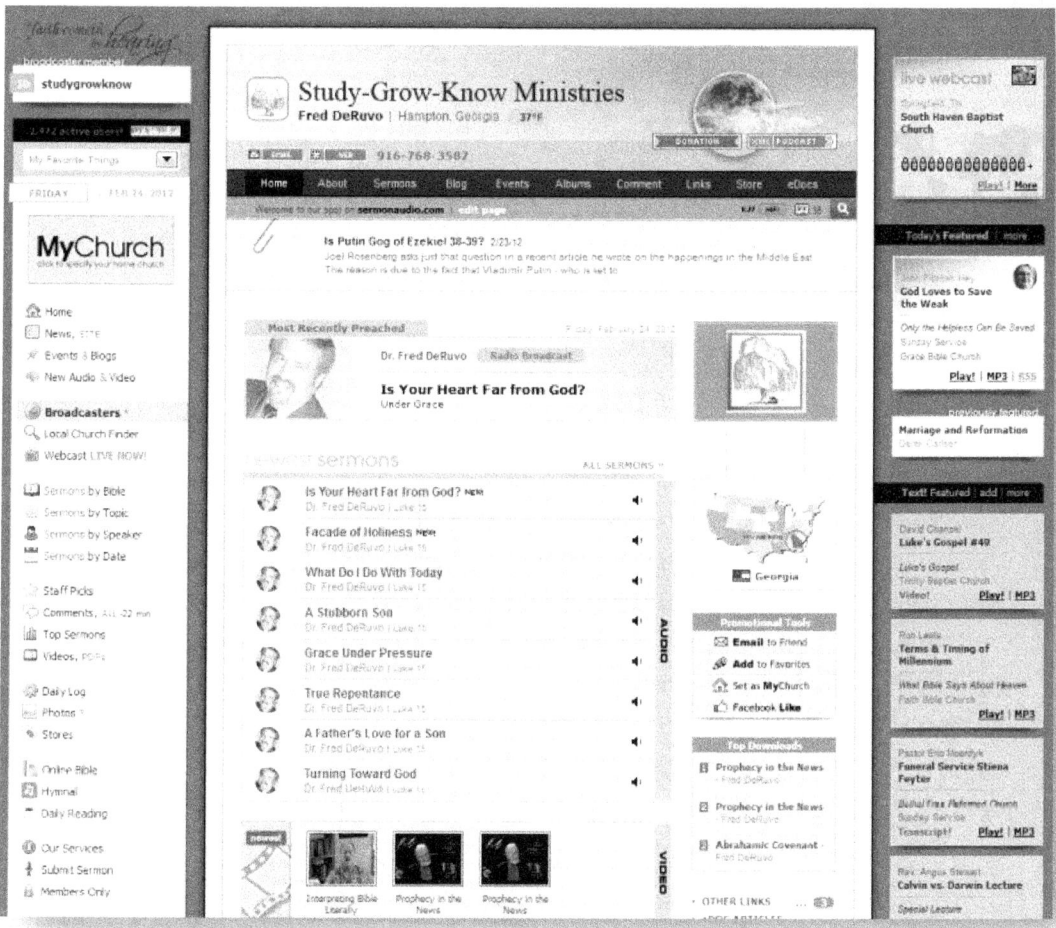

Those who understand the Bible in literal terms are constantly accused of not understanding the Bible in literal terms.

Someone will point to the word "all" or "this" or "that" and charge that the Literalist does not take those words literally, therefore they do not truly understand the Bible in literal terms.

Is there any truth to this? Does the Literalist strive to understand the literal meaning of the Bible, and by doing so, is he required to understand every word in its most literal sense? ($12.99; 142 pages, ISBN: 978-1441487568)

Christians should always be ready to present the reason for the hope that we have in Christ. However, this is completely different than attempting to win people with arguments and words. What we often fail to remember is that the Holy Spirit is deeply involved in the process of saving souls. We need to rely less on ourselves, and more on Him. Either He opens eyes, or He does not.

($11.99; 124 pages, ISBN: 978-0977424467)

Being a Christian is not necessarily a walk in the park. While it begins with the new birth Jesus spoke about with Nicodemus (John 3), this is just the starting point of a lifetime of setting Self's will to the side in favor of fulfilling Christ's will.

($10.99; 100 pages, ISBN: 978-1442110908)

You have to wonder sometimes. Though the visible church is being overrun by Contemplative Prayer, Church Growth movements, Seeker-Sensitive thinking, the Emergent Church, Spiritual Formation and a host of dangerous philosophies that are squelching the authentic gospel with what Paul would call "another" gospel, there are far too many individuals who seem unable to see the forest for the trees. ($13.99; 204 pages, ISBN: 978-0982644317)

Many think they know Dispensationalism and many believe it to be heretical, with some even viewing it as a cult. What is the truth about normative Dispensationalism? This book addresses some of the charges against it in question and short answer format.

($13.99; 194 pages, ISBN: 978-1448632404)

Because of the nature of the times we live in, it is natural to discuss areas of Eschatology (study of End Times). So many events and situations seem to point to the fact that the Tribulation period is right around the corner. During these discussions, all aspects of the End Times are routinely examined, including the timing of the Rapture, the arrival of the Antichrist, the Millennial Reign of Jesus, the coming Gog-Magog (Attempted) Invasion of Israel, and the list goes on. ($13.99; 152 pages, ISBN: 978-0982644386)

A phenomenon is happening today at an alarming rate. More and more people are boldly proclaiming that they are no longer Christians but "ex-Christians." Many are now, in fact, atheists.

Can this be true? If they are non-Christians now, were they truly Christians to begin with? They will state without equivocation that they were in fact committed Christians, but no longer are. What is the deal?

($14.99; 240 pages, ISBN: 978-1442100817)

It should be apparent to every believer that God has one supreme, overarching purpose for everything He does. Every plan He puts in motion, whether directly or by allowing it to occur, is done with that ultimate, singular purpose in mind. The natural question then becomes, what is God's singular highest purpose for everything He has accomplished, is accomplishing, or will accomplish? Is it found in the plan of redemption?   ($14.99; 224 pages, ISBN: 978-1442163676)

Four verses in the ninth chapter of Daniel are arguably some of the most important verses related to prophecy found anywhere in Scripture. If we are to understand what God has given us in these four verses then we had better do all that we can to ensure we have a correct interpretation.

The 70 weeks of Daniel, highlighted in Daniel 9:24-27, are there for our benefit. God did not need to tell us anything, but He chose to do so in order that we would be blessed by the information He has graciously provided to Daniel through the angel Gabriel.

($10.99; 77 pages, ISBN: 978-1442189546)

Rather than simply attempting to deal with aspects of this subject which have already been dealt with, author Fred DeRuvo tackles the claims against the PreTrib Rapture from another perspective.

He deals with the plausibility of a few men being able to pull off what has got to be the greatest hoax the church has ever known…if it actually was a hoax. Beyond this, DeRuvo also deals with many other claims by the Anti-PreTrib Rapturist, finding out if these claims hold any water at all.   ($13.99; 168 pages, ISBN: 978-0982644300)

There is huge disagreement about just exactly how Christians are to view their own sin. Some say there needs to be a continual awareness of how bad we are because of our sin and that we need to express absolute remorse to God whenever we commit a sin. If we do not, then God will not take us seriously and sin will not be forgiven.

($11.99; 136 pages, ISBN: 978-0983700647)

What is it that causes people to want to know the secret things of the universe, whether they are true or not? Clearly, knowledge is power, and power can feel absolute when it is kept within a cloistered group.

It appears as though there has been a deliberately hidden, yet clear, goal, known only to those who have been initiated within the various esoteric societies that have existed throughout the ages. These societies use secrecy to draw in those who seek power and dominion over the entire earth through coming cataclysmic changes. ($13.99; 182 pages, ISBN: 978-0983700661)

There is a chaos coming that is predicated upon the rise of Islam, Satanic Soldiers, aliens, and evil beyond measure. As an ideology, Islam masquerades as a religious light to the world, one that promises to usher in world peace – but at what cost? Through the use of political strategies, military might, and religious tenets, adherents of Islam work within various established governments to create special laws or exemptions for Muslims in the hope of eventually overthrowing that established government. Can it happen? IS it happening? Find out in *Evil Rising*. ($13.95; 184 pages, ISBN: 978-0977424429)

We hear all the time how bad things are getting throughout the world. Do we chalk it all up to being the normal cycles that occur in life, or is something else going on behind the scenes? What if this generation alive now turns out to be the last one before Jesus returns? Is there any truth at all to the claim that Jesus will return one day? If you are one who has not taken the time to read through some of the books of the Bible that are said to teach truths regarding the last days, *Living in the Last Generation* puts it out there in a straightforward manner, making it easy to understand. ($11.95; 132 pages, ISBN: 978-0977424405)

ALIENology is somewhat of a science for many who believe that entities from other planets or dimensions enter and leave our dimensions at will. What can we learn from these beings? Anything truthful? Dr. Fred believes that putting our faith in anything these beings say may be a huge leap in the wrong direction. Aliens reportedly come in all shapes, sizes, and even cultural representations. Because of this, there tends to be a good deal of mixed messages out there, yet people believe it because of their experience. Anything wrong with that picture? ($14.99; 176 pages, ISBN: 978-0983700609)

Raised for His Glory delves into the books of Ezekiel and Romans to determine what the Bible actually says about Israel. Is the section on Ezekiel 36-39 speaking of a future time when nations will gather against Israel, or is this something that has already occurred? Moreover, just exactly what is the Valley of the Dry Bones referring to – the nation of Israel, or the Church? Join Dr. Fred as he presents his understanding of these very important sections of God's Word and how they relate to the only nation that He ever created, *Israel*. ($15.99; 190 pages, ISBN: 978-0983700623)

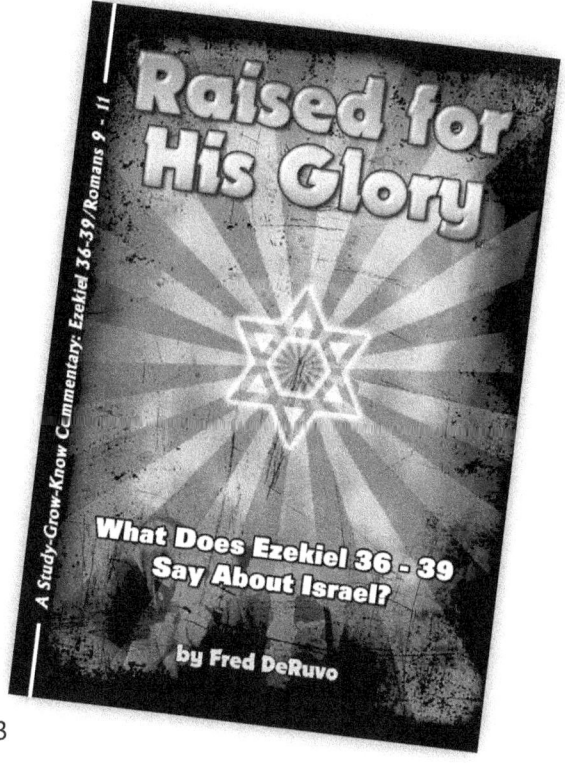

Society has changed drastically over the past decades. Why is that? Simply due to the fact that people have become more preoccupied with *Self*. In this book, Dr. Fred presents *Self* as an entity capable of getting things done its way and using the individual to accomplish it.

In essence, Self easily becomes the master to every person who is not under the control of God's Holy Spirit, with the person becoming the slave. ($14.99; 206 pages, ISBN: 978-0983700630)

In this commentary on Revelation, author Fred DeRuvo draws back the curtain on chapters five through twenty-two, presenting information in an easy-to-understand style, written for the average person. One thing is certain regarding the book of Revelation. Because of its prophetic nature, Christians will continue to debate aspects of it until such a time as we can know for certain. Either the things found within Revelation are yet to come to pass, and that alone will prove their veracity, or they will not come to *pass. Only time will tell.* ($18.00; 392 pages, ISBN: 978-0977424498)

The book of Jude is only twenty-five verses in length, but it packs a spiritual wallop! Jude, the brother of James (and half-brother of our Lord Jesus), writes a message to believers about the times in which they lived. Those times are not at all that much different from the days in which we now live. Jude warns against apostasy, licentiousness, and the mockers that are destined to be part of the last days. Even during Jude's day, mocking the Lord's return had already begun. How much worse is it today, roughly 2,000 years later? ($11.99; 126 pages, ISBN: 978-0983700692)

Everyone has an opinion. It does not matter whether you're a New Ager, a UFO researcher, a student of the Bible, or simply a curious party. Theories regarding aliens range from believing that the whole alien phenomenon is nothing more than an elaborate hoax, to the belief that they are real and getting ready to take over our world, to the view that they are demons disguising themselves as aliens.

($15.99; 206 pages, ISBN: 978-0982644393)

Chrislam

Moo!

www.ingramcontent.com/pod-product-compliance
Lightning Source LLC
LaVergne TN
LVHW081354060426
835510LV00013B/1810